Mapping

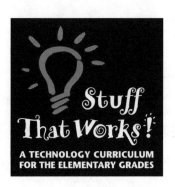

Stuff That Works!

A TECHNOLOGY CURRICULUM
FOR THE ELEMENTARY GRADES

Mapping

Gary Benenson and James L. Neujahr
Project Directors, City Technology

Heinemann
Portsmouth, NH

Heinemann
A division of Reed Elsevier Inc.
361 Hanover Street
Portsmouth, NH 03801–3912
www.heinemann.com

Offices and agents throughout the world

Stuff That Works!
City College of New York
140 Street & Convent Avenue, Room T233
New York, New York 10031
(212) 650-8389 tel.; (212) 650-8013 fax
citytechnology@ccny.cuny.edu

This project was supported, in part, by the
National Science Foundation
Opinions expressed are those of the authors and not necessarily those of the Foundation

Project Staff
Gary Benenson, *Project Director, City College of New York, School of Engineering*
James L. Neujahr, *Project Co-Director, City College of New York, School of Education*
Dorothy Bennett, *Education Development Center/Center for Children and Technology*
Terri Meade, *Education Development Center/Center for Children and Technology*

Advisory Board
William Barowy, *Lesley College*
David Chapin, *City University of New York*
Alan Feigenberg, *City College of New York*

Ed Goldman, *Brooklyn Technical High School*
Patricia Hutchinson, *The College of New Jersey*
Neville Parker, *City College of New York*
Peter Sellwood, *Consultant, United Kingdom*
Ron Todd, *The College of New Jersey*

Production Staff
Gary Benenson, *General Editor*
James L. Neujahr and Gary Benenson, *Lead Authors*
Lorin Driggs, *Editor*
Doris Halle Design NYC, *Design and Graphics*
Maria Politarhos, *Photography*
Juana Maria Page, *Illustrations*

Teacher Associates/Coauthors
Linda Crews, *PS 84, New York, NY*
Helen deCandido, *Retired*
Mary Flores, *CES 42, Bronx, NY*
Angel Gonzalez, *Family Academy, New York, NY*
Michael Gatton, *IS 143M, New York, NY*
Sandra Jenoure, *PS 155, New York, NY*
Danell Pankas, *Berkeley Bunker, Las Vegas, NV*
Felice Piggott, *PS 145, New York, NY*
Annette Purnell, *CES 42, Bronx, NY*
Minerva Rivera, *Harbor Academy, New York, NY*

Library of Congress Cataloging-in-Publication Data
Benenson, Gary.
    Stuff that works! : a technology curriculum for the elementary grades / Gary Benenson and James L. Neujahr.
        p. cm.
    Includes bibliographical references.
    Contents: [v. 5] Mapping
    ISBN 0-325-00467-6
    1. Technology—Study and Teaching(Elementary)—United States.   I. Neujahr, James L., 1939– .   II. Title.
T72 .B46 2002
372.3′5—dc21   2001059398

Printed in the United States of America on acid-free paper

06   05   04   03   VP   2   3   4   5

CONTENTS

FOREWORD

IN A WORLD INCREASINGLY DEPENDENT ON TECHNOLOGY—where new ideas and tools pervade our personal and civic lives and where important choices hinge on our knowledge of how things and people work—the imperative that all students should learn to understand and use technology well should be obvious. Yet in the American curriculum, still overstuffed with tradition and trivia, there is little room in the day for learning and teaching about important ideas from technology and very few resources for educators who want to engage their students in learning for the 21st century.

Stuff That Works! is a groundbreaking curriculum. It provides a set of carefully chosen and designed activities that will engage elementary students with the core ideas and processes of technology (or engineering, if you prefer). Elementary school is the ideal place to begin learning about technology. It is a time in students' development when they are ready and eager to take on concrete rather than abstract ideas. The concepts and skills presented in

Stuff That Works! will support more advanced learning in mathematics, science, and technology as students move up through the grades.

But there is much more to *Stuff That Works!* than a set of activities. As a matter of fact, the activities make up less than a third of the pages. *Stuff That Works!* also includes helpful resources for the teacher such as clear discussions of the important ideas and skills from technology that their students should be learning; stories of how the materials have been used in real classrooms; suggestions for outside reading; guidance for assessing how well their students are doing; and tips on implementation. I hope teachers will take time to make full use of these valuable resources as they use *Stuff That Works!* If they do, they can help their students take the first, critical steps towards technological literacy and success in and beyond school.

George D. Nelson, Director
*American Association for
the Advancement of Science (AAAS)
Project 2061*

INTRODUCTION

What Is Technology?

Stuff That Works! Mapping will introduce you to a novel and very engaging approach to the study of technology at the elementary school level. In education today, the word technology is most often associated with learning how to use computers, and that is certainly important. But learning how to use a particular kind of technology is not the same thing as learning how and why the technology works. Children learn about computers as users rather than as students of how computers work or of how to design them. In fact, computer analysis and design require technical knowledge that is beyond most adults, let alone elementary-aged children. Fortunately, there are many other examples of technology that are much more accessible than computers and that present many of the same issues as computers and other "high-tech" devices.

The purpose of technology is to solve practical problems by means of devices, systems, procedures, and environments that improve people's lives in one way or another. Understood this way, a computer is no more an example of technology than...

- the cardboard box it was shipped in,
- the arrangement of the computer and its peripherals on the table,
- the symbol next to the printer's ON/OFF switch,
- or the ballpoint pen the printer replaces as a writing device.

A box, a plan for the use of table space, an ON/OFF symbol, and a pen are examples of technologies you and your students will explore in this and the other *Stuff That Works!* guides.

The *Stuff That Works!* approach is based on artifacts and systems that are all around us and available for free or at very low cost. You need not be a technical guru or rich in resources to engage yourself and your students in technology. The activities in *Mapping* are grounded in a broad range of experiences that are part of children's everyday world. These experiences include making sense of maps—whether of museums, transportation systems, or state and nation. They also include creating maps to assist in planning, explaining, or giving directions.

Why Study Technology in Elementary School?

Below is a graphic summary of the process of "doing" technology as we present it in this book. The study of technology challenges students to identify and solve problems, build understanding, develop and apply competence and knowledge in a variety of processes and content areas, including science, mathematics, language arts, and social interaction.

The teachers who field-tested these materials underscored that these activities helped their students to:

• observe and describe phenomena in detail;

• explore real objects and situations by creating models and other representations;

• identify salient aspects of problems;

• solve authentic problems;

• use evidence-based reasoning;

• apply the scientific method;

• ask thoughtful questions;

• communicate in oral, written, and graphic form;

• collaborate effectively with others.

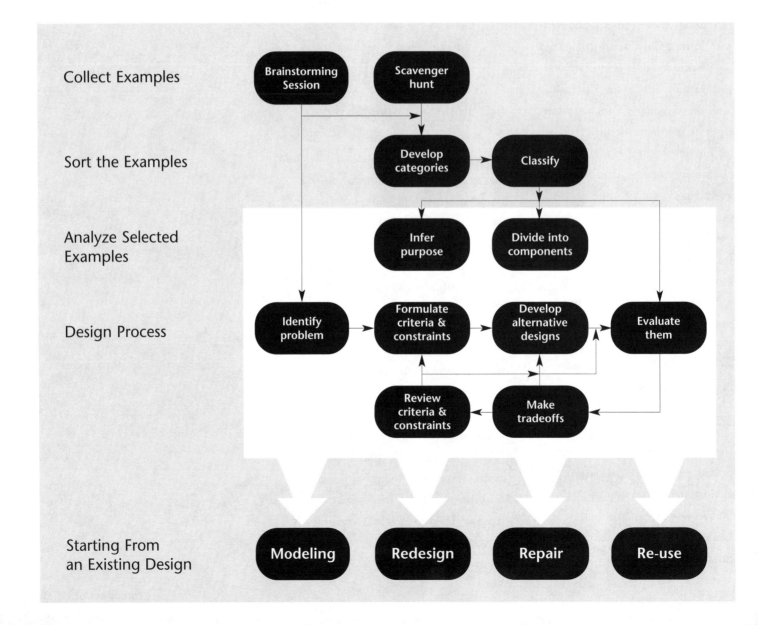

Educational Goals for *Mapping*

Mapping deals with two basic processes:
- obtaining meaning from graphical representations of physical spaces and
- creating graphical representations of physical spaces to communicate one's own meanings to others.

The content and activities presented here will help you meet these goals:

- Develop fundamental themes of two-dimensional representation of three-dimensional space;
- Illustrate and explore concepts of orienting, symbol use, point of view, scale, and one-to-one correspondences;
- Demystify common artifacts, and by extension, technology in general;

- Promote literacy as students interpret and develop graphic communications;
- Develop process skills in observation, classification, ordering, inferring, collecting and organizing data, representing data, design, and evaluation;
- Provide rich opportunities for group work.

How This Guide Is Organized

Each *Stuff That Works!* guide is organized into the following chapters.

Chapter 1. *Appetizers* suggests some things you can do for yourself, to become familiar with the topic. You can do these activities at home, using only found materials. They will help you to recognize some of the technology that is all around you, and offer ways of making sense of it.

Chapter 2. *Concepts* develops the main ideas that can be taught for and through the topic. These include ideas from science, math, social studies and art, as well as technology.

Chapter 3. *Activities* contains a variety of classroom projects and units related to the topic, including those referred to in Chapter 4. Each activity includes prerequisites, goals, skills and concepts; materials, references to standards and teacher tips; and sample worksheets.

Chapter 4. *Stories* presents teachers' narratives about what happened in their own classrooms. Their accounts include photos, samples of children's work and children's dialog. Commentary by project staff connects the teachers' accounts with the concepts developed in Chapter 2.

Chapter 5. *Resources* provides a framework supporting the implementation of the activities. It includes an annotated bibliography of children's literature and a discussion of assessment opportunities.

Chapter 6. *About Standards* shows how the activities and ideas in this book address national standards in technology, science, math, English language arts (ELA), and social studies.

How to Use This Guide

Different teachers will obviously come to this book with different needs and objectives. However, regardless of your background, instructional approach, and curricular goals, *we strongly recommend that you begin with Chapter 1, "Appetizers."* There is simply no better way to become acquainted with a topic and to understand what your students will be facing than to try out some of the ideas and activities for yourself. Chapter 1 guides you through that process.

The content and approach presented in *Mapping* are based on the premise that processes of design are central to the practice of technology, just as inquiry is the central activity of science. While no two design problems are the same, there are some features that characterize any design task:

- It should solve a problem of some sort.
- It must have more than one possible solution.
- There must be an effort to test the design.

A problem is like a trigger that initiates a design process. Often the problem is not well-formulated, a vague kind of "wouldn't it be nice if …" In making the problem more specific, it is often helpful to list some criteria the design must address. In trying to satisfy these criteria, the designer is never completely free to do whatever he or she wants. There are always constraints, which could involve cost, safety, ease of use, and a host of other considerations.

There is no one way to do design. It is a non-linear, messy process that typically begins with very incomplete information. Additional criteria become apparent as the design is implemented and tested. New constraints appear that were not originally evident. It is often necessary to backtrack and revise the original specifications. Such a messy process may seem contrary to the work you usually expect to see happening in your classroom. However, we encourage you to embrace the messiness! It will justify itself by improving students' competence in reasoning, problem-solving, and ability to communicate not only what they are doing but also why they are doing it and what results they expect.

$\mathcal{A}$ Brief History of *Stuff That Works!*

The guides in the *Stuff That Works!* series were developed through collaboration among three different kinds of educators:

- Two college professors, one from the School of Education of City College of the City University of New York, and the other from the City College School of Engineering;
- Two educational researchers from the Center for Children and Technology of the Education Development Center (CCT/ EDC);
- Thirty New York City elementary educators who work in the South Bronx, Harlem, and Washington Heights.

This last group included science specialists, early childhood educators, special education teachers, a math specialist, a language arts specialist, and regular classroom teachers from grades two through seven. In teaching experience, they ranged from first-year teachers to veterans with more than 20 years in the classroom.

During the 1997-98 and 1998-99 academic years, the teachers participated in workshops that engaged them in sample activities and also provided opportunities for sharing and discussion of classroom experiences. The work-shop activities then became the basis

for classroom implementation. The teachers were encouraged to modify the workshop activities and extend them in accordance with their own teaching situations, their ideas, and their children's interests.

The teachers, project staff, and the research team collaborated to develop a format for documenting classroom outcomes in the form of portfolios. These portfolios included the following items:

- lesson worksheets describing the activities and units implemented in the classroom, including materials used, teacher tips and strategies, and assessment methods;
- narrative descriptions of what actually happened in the classroom;
- samples of students' work, includ-ing writing, maps and drawings, and dialogue; and
- the teachers' own reflections on the activities.

The lesson worksheets became the basis for the **Activities** (Chapter 3) of each guide. The narratives, samples of student work, and teacher reflections formed the core of the **Stories** (Chapter 4). At the end of the two years of curriculum development and pilot testing, the project produced five guides in draft form.

During the 1999-2000 academic year, the five draft guides were field-tested at five sites, including two in New York City, one suburban New York site, and one each in Michigan and Nevada. To prepare for the field tests, two staff developers from each site attended a one-week summer institute, to familiarize themselves with the guides and engage in sample workshop activities. During the subsequent academic year, the staff developers carried out workshops at their home sites to introduce the guides to teachers in their regions. These workshops lasted from two to three hours per topic. From among the workshop participants, the staff developers recruited teachers to field-test the *Stuff That Works!* activities in their own classrooms and to evaluate the guides. Data from these field tests then became the basis for major revisions that are reflected in the current versions of all five guides.

Chapter 1

ÁPPÉTiZÉRS

Map Your Desk

Made any maps lately? Your desk is fairly self-contained, and probably very familiar and important to you. Before you proceed to the next paragraph, we urge you to make a map of your own desk. You can do it from memory or while sitting at it. An ordinary sheet of 8-1/2" x 11" paper is fine for this purpose. If available, a piece of grid paper can make it easier to lay things out and draw lines. Your map need not be fancy or precise, but it should show all the major areas and artifacts on your desk.

Mapping your desk can be a remarkably useful exercise. We have asked several dozen teachers and other adults, including ourselves, to make desk maps. A majority (again, including ourselves) has subsequently decided to rearrange these workspaces. Mapping is a way to collect and present data that often leads to changes in the subject under study.

Jennifer's desk, for example, is divided into regions surrounded by empty space. (See Figure 1-1.) Most desks are considerably more cluttered. Even so, there is an element of self-reflection in the label, "Do-it-later Pile," which is in contrast with "Today's Work." Subsequently, she redesigned her desk to use two trays labeled "Important" and "Sort Later." This is an example of how a map can serve as a tool for redesign. Analysis and design of spaces such as desks are discussed in detail in the *Stuff That Works!* guide, *Designed Environments: Places, Practices, and Plans.*

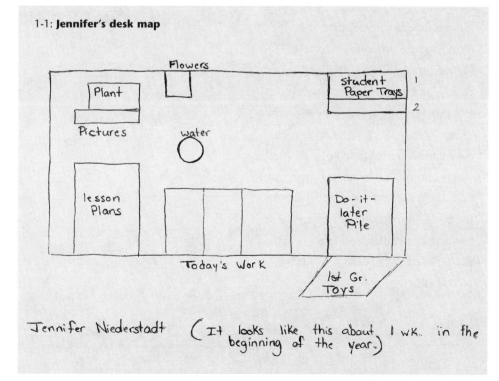

1-1: **Jennifer's desk map**

Jennifer's map is only one kind of desk map. Dorothy, an educational researcher, made the desk map shown in Figure 1-2. Comparing Dorothy's map with Jennifer's, several major differences are obvious:

- Dorothy represents the various areas of her desk by drawing them, as well as labeling them;
- She has interpreted "desk" broadly to include considerable space around her desk; and
- Her map shows the drawers as well as the top of the desk.

Both Dorothy and Jennifer were asked simply to "map your desk," but their interpretations are very different. Neither one is "better" than the other, and neither one is "correct." Depending on the purpose, either of these maps might be more useful. For this reason, we urge you to do the "Map Your Desk" activity with a colleague or friend. Each of you should map your own desk independently, and then compare maps afterwards. Look for both similarities and differences in the two maps. Based on looking at the other map, how would you change your own?

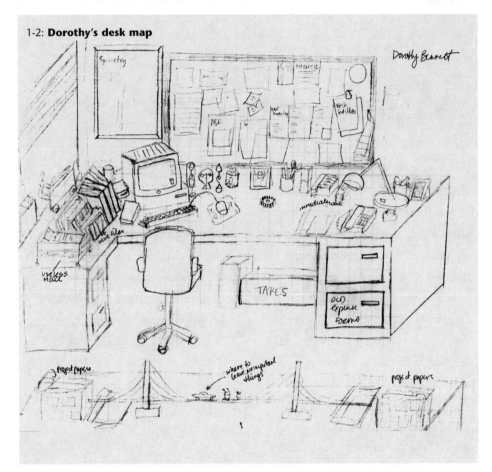

1-2: **Dorothy's desk map**

Route Maps

A visitor to your classroom wants to find the cafeteria. You could describe the route in words, but a map would be much more compact and easier to follow. Make a route map showing the visitor the way from your classroom to the cafeteria. Then try your map out with a visitor who really doesn't know the way.

- What problems did the visitor have?
- How would you redesign your map to make it easier to follow?
- What assumptions did you make about the audience for your map?

Figure 1-3 is a map showing how to get from the office area to the classroom. The map uses a number of common graphic elements. In the original map, the floors (1st and 2nd) are distinguished from each other using a code of solid and dashed lines. Some "landmarks" are identified, such as "Entrance" and "Office." Symbols are used to indicate stairs and doors, and a key at the top explains the meaning of these symbols. Arrows are used to show direction of travel. Some of these graphic elements are so common and obvious as to seem "natural," but they are not the only ones that could have been used. For example, some souvenir maps use footprints instead

of arrows to show direction. Numerous design choices went into this (or any) map.

A teacher (the map-writer) made the map in Figure 1-3 as part of a workshop on mapping. Visitors (the map-readers) who were unfamiliar with the building then tried to follow it. All found the destination easily although some took the stairway across from the office rather than the one indicated. Like any other form of communication, maps require interpretation. There is rarely a perfect match between the meaning as intended and the meaning as received. If the map-reader gets lost, the mismatch is pretty serious, and the map should probably be redesigned!

1-3: Route map: office to room 214

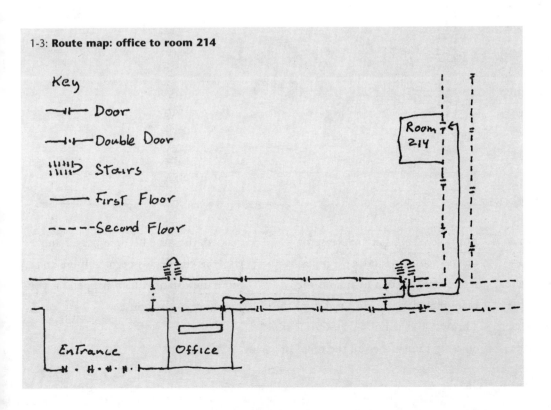

Imagine that you've invited company to your house, but they don't know where you live. Should you provide directions in words or on a map? The map might be clearer, because it provides visual clues to what the route looks like. Make a map showing someone how to get to your house. Figure 1-4 shows a typical route map of this sort. Like the map in Figure 1-3, it contains landmarks and symbols. It assumes that the reader is starting from "NYC" (New York City), has a car, and can find the Thruway.

A variety of symbols are used on this map: two parallel lines for the highway, a circle with an "x" inside for a traffic light, and a rectangle for a city block. Figure 1-4 also uses another common feature of maps—coordinate systems. One coordinate system is suggested by the exit number on the Thruway; "second light" and "three blocks" in the more detailed section imply other uses of coordinates. In one respect, an outdoor route map is simpler than most building maps, because there is no third dimension to worry about.

Unlike the other maps discussed so far, the map in Figure 1-4 makes no attempt to maintain a consistent scale. In other words, equal distances on the map do not necessarily represent equal distances in the real world. The distance

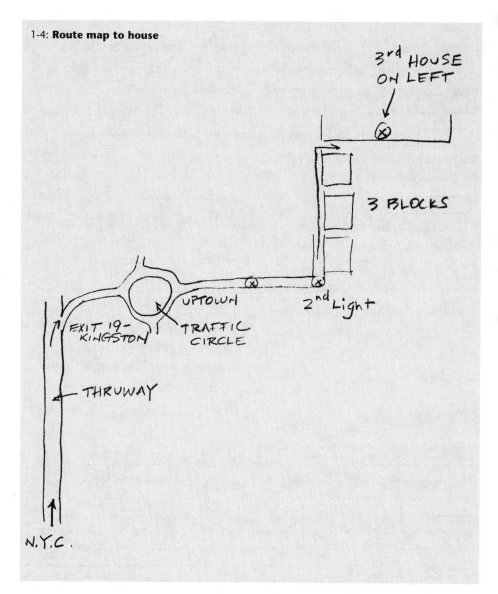

1-4: **Route map to house**

from New York City to Kingston on the Thruway, about 90 miles, is represented by two inches on the map. However, the distance from the Thruway to the house, about one mile, takes up four inches on the map. In

general, the scale becomes larger and larger as the details become more and more important, which happens as you get closer to the house.

ℬad Maps

Have you encountered maps that are misleading or difficult to follow? What aspects of the maps create these problems? How would you redesign them to make them work better? It is very useful to examine these carefully to discover where they went wrong. By analyzing the problems in other people's maps, you can avoid the same problems in your own.

Figure 1-5 shows a floor plan that is posted at many locations in the North Academic Center of City College. The map shown in Figure 1-5 is posted on the wall adjacent to the elevators.

As you stand in front of the map, the elevators are immediately to the left. But according to the map, they should be on your right. The map is hard to follow because right and left on the map do not correspond at all to right and left in real space. Similarly, what is at the top of the map is not ahead of you, as you would expect, but behind. A simple solution to this problem would be to rotate the map through 180 degrees. It would then be properly oriented to the surroundings, although the words would be upside down.

1-5: Sign with floor plan (left) and close-up of floor plan (right)

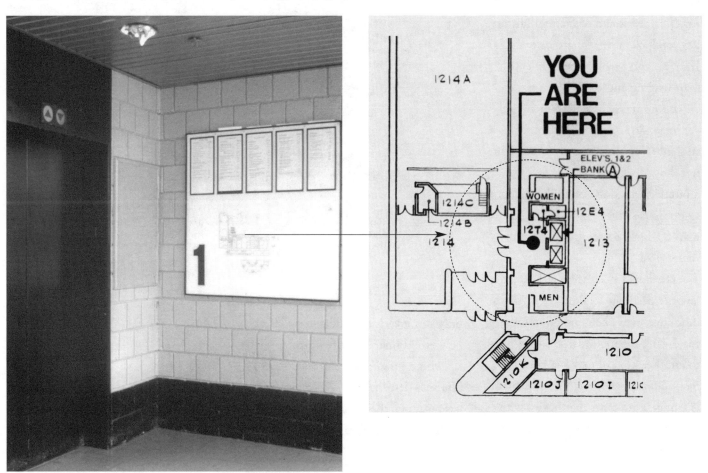

$\mathcal{A}$ Mapping Inventory

Make a survey of the maps in your own life. What do you use them for? Which ones are the most useful, and why? When you go on vacation, what role do maps play? Are there any maps you enjoy particularly? Do you have any "bad maps"?

If you are a classroom teacher, you probably take your class on some trips. Most of the places you would go, such as museums, zoos, and parks, probably offer free visitor maps, such as the one in Figure 1-6 of the Fossil Halls of the American Museum of Natural History. Do you look at these maps beforehand? If so, do you involve your students in map-reading and route-planning, or do you do it all yourself? When you get there, do you obtain a map for each student? Can they follow the map? If not, how do students find their way around? What do you tell the children to do, in case they get lost? Would map-reading be useful to them on these trips?

The Fossil Halls (Figure 1-6) are a favorite destination: they are where the dinosaurs live. The orientation center for this new exhibit introduces visitors to another kind of map—a *cladogram* or *evolutionary diagram*. The cladogram is a branching chart that begins with precursors of the dinosaurs. The chart

1-6: **Visitor's map of Fossil Halls of the American Museum of Natural History**
©American Museum of Natural History. *Used with permission.*

branches at each point that a significant new evolutionary feature develops that is common to a particular line of dinosaur descendents. The museum has organized the Fossil Halls according to this evolutionary diagram.

A Small Sample of New York City Maps

A wide variety of maps is likely to be available for your region. Even though they may represent the same physical space, different maps show different kinds of information. To illustrate the kinds of information that can be shown on a map, we have collected a group of maps of New York City and its surroundings. Each of these maps was designed with a different audience in mind and for different purposes. Although only a small portion of each map is shown, each map shows roughly the same territory; however, the information on them is very different.

Road Map

The AAA road map to Manhattan (Figure 1-7) is designed for those who visit by car. It is drawn to scale. Almost all streets are shown, as are tourist destinations including landmarks, restaurants, and hotels.

1-7: **Lower Manhattan—road map.** © AAA. *Used by permission.*

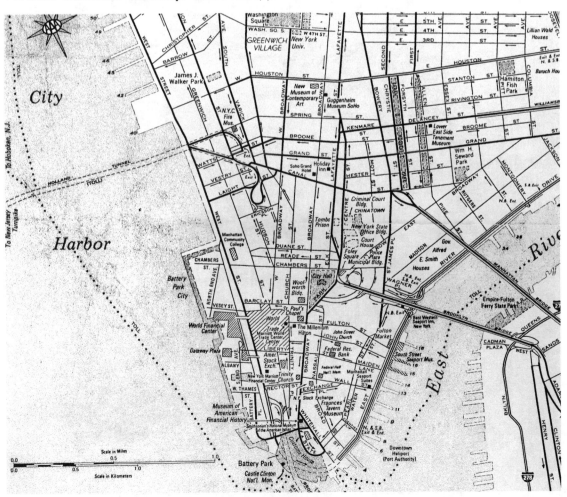

Bus and Subway Map

This New York City Transit Authority map shows bus and subway routes in Lower Manhattan. It shows major streets and destinations to orient those traveling by public transportation.

1-8: **Lower Manhattan—bus and subway map.**
© Metropolitan Transportation Authority. *Used by permission.*

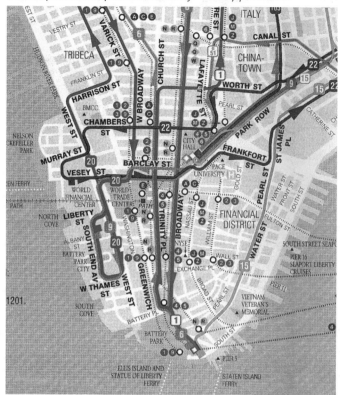

1-9: **Lower Manhattan—artistic rendering**

Panoramic Drawing

Here is an artistic rendering of Lower Manhattan and its surroundings. Unlike the typical "bird's-eye view" map, this map conveys the heights of various buildings. It is a view that visitors and residents rarely (if ever) see, although the landmarks themselves are familiar.

Guidebook and Map in One

Here is another aerial view of Manhattan, but this time the intent is to provide visitors, particularly families, with very useful information about tourist spots. Its intended audience is the pedestrian; it includes no information on public transportation or access routes for those visiting by car. Produced by MapEasy, this not only provides tourist information, but its drawings allow the walker to identify major buildings.

1-10: **Midtown Manhattan—guidebook and map in one.**
© MapEasy, Inc. *Used by permission.*

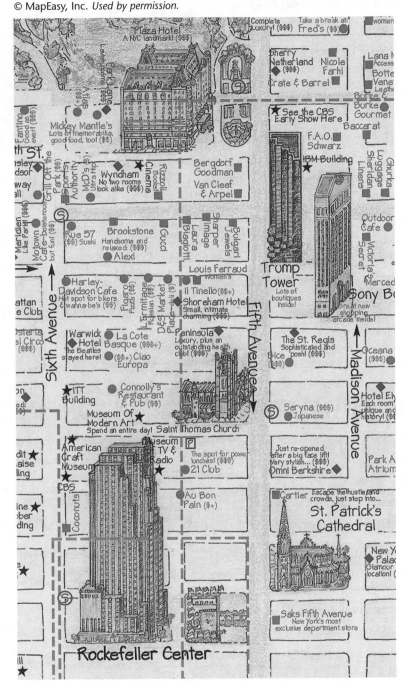

Aerial Photograph

These days, most professional maps are constructed from aerial photographs, which raises the question: What does a map show that an aerial photograph doesn't? Figure 1-11 is an example of an aerial photograph of the City College campus, in Upper Manhattan, running from south-southwest at the bottom to north-northeast at the top. An athletic field is seen near the southern end of the campus, several college buildings are to the north, and St. Nicholas Park is the wooded area to the right. Nothing on this photograph is labeled, and there is little information on the landscape features.

Topographical Map

Figure 1-12 is a view of Upper Manhattan that includes the City College campus (light rectangular area near the center) shown in the aerial photograph in Figure 1-11. It also includes the location of many public buildings. A map like this could be very useful in beginning to think about mapping the neighborhood of the school. USGS topo maps are available for the entire country. (A web address with further information is included below under "Making Your Own Map Collection.") Note how close the contour lines are in St. Nicholas Park (center), indicating a steep slope. This feature of the landscape is not at all evident from the aerial photograph (Figure 1-11).

1-11: Upper Manhattan—aerial photograph of City College (photo by Phil Carvalho)

1-12: Upper Manhattan—U.S. Geological Survey topographical map

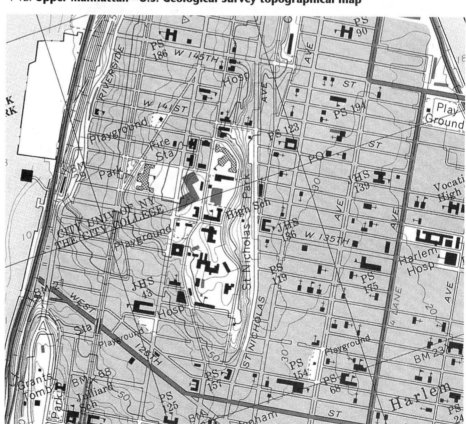

Making Your Own Map Collection

Maps are all around. There are bus maps, road maps, and floor plans for museums. There are weather maps, star maps, and maps of theaters and stadiums. Many of these maps are free, so be sure to collect them for your class. Some of the sources for free maps are newspapers, telephone books, rest stops along interstate highways, and state and local tourism offices. The front of our local phone book has seating plans for sports facilities and theaters, as well as street maps of the area. The phone book also has a local zip code map and a map showing area codes and time zones across the United States. Other free maps include guides to exhibits at museums and guides to national parks, monuments, and historical sites. Also be on the lookout for aerial photographs, especially of your town or neighborhood. Sometimes you can even find someone who is disposing of old *National Geographic* magazines.

The Internet has become the best source of maps and map information. The best guide to Web resources that we have found is at http://www.nationalgeographic.com/. The National Geographic homepage itself has a wealth of information. This page is regularly updated with items of particular interest, so visit it often. The "For Teachers" section is of particular interest. Go there and you will find a gateway to all sorts of interesting resources for mapping.

Not all maps are free. We buy maps at stationery shops, bookstores, and tourism centers. The best topographic maps are those produced by the U.S. Geological Survey (USGS). The U.S. Geological Survey home page, at http://mapping.usgs.gov/, tells you how to obtain these maps. It includes a master map showing the territory covered by each map, information on ordering single copies directly from USGS, and the addresses of local dealers who carry them. It also contains information on maps of other parts of the world.

Finally, don't forget the obvious. You probably already have atlases, social studies texts, globes, and other sources of maps. Use them. Combine them with the rich collection of maps you have gathered from other sources. Children will see that mapping is not a school subject limited to texts, but that the texts have the same kinds of maps people use in their everyday lives.

Preparing the Way for Mapping in Your School

Mapping is a "hands-on" curriculum with no kit of supplies. This means that you may need help in assembling the necessary materials—they are commonplace and free, but may not be readily at hand. When your children are analyzing spaces beyond your classroom, enlist the cooperation and assistance you need from your principal, the school custodian, and parents first, just as you do with other active learning projects.

Some of the projects use materials that are found in the school's waste stream. The main example of this is cardboard. Schools generate large amounts of cardboard waste. It ends up with the custodian before going to a recycler or garbage collector. Custodians are usually happy to help, if they know in advance what you want and why. Tell them about the projects you are planning. You may find that they can help with far more than just access to cardboard. A custodian may be able to help you find storage space beyond your classroom, provide you with blueprints of the school or maps of the school grounds, and suggest unexplored areas of the building for mapping projects.

Parents can also provide invaluable resources, especially if you enlist their support early in the planning stages. Some parents may have access to specialized maps through their jobs or community activities. They can also help you and the children collect recycled materials for use in the classroom. Mapping projects often involve spaces in the home or community—such as "Map Your Room" or "Map Your Block"—and parents can be essential in facilitating these activities. Parent volunteers are especially important as assistants when you have projects that take your class outside the school building.

Finally, there is the principal. Principals can make or break a project-centered approach to teaching and learning. They do this through control over room assignments, scheduling, rules, and procedures. At the very least you need to have your principal's acceptance of what you plan. Sharing your plans is the first step. A second step may be to point out the public relations aspect of what you are doing. Parental involvement in the project may help. Design projects that improve the appearance of the school may also receive the principal's support. It is important to let the principal know the variety of outcomes that may come from the project.

In the various things you do to garner support for a project, remember that the children are usually the best advocates. If they are excited about what they are doing, it is much harder for adults to say no.

Chapter 2
CONCEPTS

Why Do Mapping?

Many adults are intimidated by maps, while many others find them intriguing. Some motorists negotiate their way without ever looking at a map, while others pore over them, painstakingly constructing the optimum route. There are "map buffs," who can spend hours examining maps of places they've never been, and who can tell you all kinds of details they've learned just from looking at maps. Even for map enthusiasts, reading maps is easier than writing them. Asked to make a map, most adults will inform you that they can't draw, and will instead struggle with words to express where a place is or how to get there. Maps evoke both fear and fascination.

In general, children like maps. They are miniature, manageable versions of the world, with some of the same characteristics as dolls and doll houses, toy cars and trucks, and other kid-sized models of things. At the same time children enjoy looking at maps, they are often confused by them. Some think that the color of a country on the map is also the color of the real country. An island must be floating, because what could be under it? They can't imagine that the physical land might not end where the map ends; or that a river could flow north, because north is represented by "up" on the map. Many relationships that map-literate adults take for granted are not at all obvious to children, nor, probably, to many adults.

ℬeyond the Three Rs

Maps are above all a means of communication. There are a variety of ways to convey ideas: through written or spoken words, sounds, numbers, two-dimensional graphics, three-dimensional models, and body movements. Traditionally, educational institutions have focused primarily on written language and numbers, as summarized by the "Three Rs." Literacy and numeracy are the primary goals of most elementary curricula. While most maps include words and numbers, they also use graphic devices to communicate. Mapping does not fit neatly in the traditional curriculum.

Are literacy and numeracy sufficient preparation for the contemporary world? Do students also need experience in speaking and listening, and in using other sound-based means of communication and expression, such as music? Should they learn to control their own body movements, to communicate by gestures, and to interpret body language? Do they need to construct three-dimensional sculptures and models, and to explore how these convey meaning? Should they learn to both "read" and "write" maps, graphs, diagrams,

Web pages, and other graphic representations? Most experts in cognitive development and practitioners of modern communication techniques would argue that all of these skills are important in education.

Graphics Wherever You Look

Here we will focus on graphic communication. Science, engineering, and architecture draw heavily on visual ways of representing ideas, data, and designs. In science, for example, the Periodic Table is a graphical way of representing the relationships among the elements, and it was basic to the development of modern chemistry. The theory of plate tectonics, originally called "continental drift," arose from the insight that the continents fit together like a jigsaw puzzle. Engineers often communicate their preliminary thinking about a problem using "back-of-the-envelope" sketches. Nearly all patent applications include extensive drawings showing what the design looks like and how it is different from prior inventions. Architects communicate with contractors and engineers primarily in the form of plans showing how the space will look.

With the rapid spread of computer technology, graphic communication has penetrated into nearly every other field as well. Businesspeople use "presentation graphics" to convince potential clients and partners; packages are adorned with graphics intended to sell the product; and graphic symbols increasingly replace words for multicultural communication. Many home appliances and furniture items now require "some assembly," and the directions nearly always depend on graphic communication.

In education, nearly every topic becomes easier to understand when graphic devices are used. Imagine trying to understand history without time lines, music without scores, or geography without maps. Diagramming sentences, while currently out of favor, was an effective way to visualize sentence structure and parts of speech; Venn diagrams express and clarify relationships among categories; and schematic diagrams are indispensable in describing even the simplest circuits. Windows and Mac operating systems have replaced DOS because they express the relationships among computer files using graphics rather than text.

Maps as an Entry to Graphic Communication

In the broad sense of mapping (discussed in detail in Chapter 4), the Periodic Table, engineering sketches, business graphs, time lines, musical scores, sentence diagrams, Venn diagrams, circuit diagrams, and computer "desktops" can all be considered maps of a sort. Each of these devices takes one kind of information and "maps" it onto two-dimensional images. For example, one note in a musical score corresponds to one sound made by an instrument. In its broader, more abstract sense, this is what a map does: it provides a one-to-one correspondence between events, things, or ideas in the real world and symbols on a page. This is what teachers mean when they talk about a *concept map.*

Most of the time, however, mapping has a much more restricted meaning. We call a diagram or drawing a *geographical map* if it represents relationships in physical space. A geographical map may be the most intuitive kind of graphic communication device, because it uses spatial relationships on the page to represent similar arrangements in real space. Mapping (in this narrower sense) is

an excellent way to open up the world of graphics. As we shall see, very young children can learn to read and write maps —sometimes before they can read and write words. Mapping is a natural way to introduce more abstract forms of graphic communication, such as graphs, Venn diagrams, concept maps, and the rest.

What Is There to Mapping?

Mapping is more than an intuitive act. Let's consider some of the things you have to do to construct a realistic map:

1. *Observe* the physical space. In order to map a space, it is necessary to look at it carefully, much more carefully than you usually do.
2. *Integrate* a series of observations into a unified whole. Most spaces are too large to view in detail all at once. Our observations of them are sequential—we see one piece at a time, followed by another piece, etc. The map-maker has to take all of these sequential observations and synchronize them so they all appear on the same map. In early mapping exercises, a teacher may eliminate this step by having students map only one object.

3. *Orient* the items on the map so they correspond with the way they are really seen from the viewpoint implied by the map. Achieving a consistent orientation can be a significant hurdle for beginners. Both children and adults tend to mix side views with top views in their first attempts at mapping. Developing a consistent viewpoint provides a natural introduction to rotation and angular measurement.
4. *Scale* the map so the items on it are proportional in size to their sizes in real life. Making a scale map presents serious problems for beginners, which can be overcome using techniques such as the "Master Map." (See Chapter 4.) Scale mapping provides a contextual entry into ratio and proportion.
5. *Use symbols* to reduce the amount of information and increase the clarity of a map. Symbolization is a key concept in all communication, whether oral, written, or graphic. Mapping offers a context for children to see the need and value of symbols and to gain experience in inventing their own.

Under What Subject Does Mapping Belong?

Do Maps Tell the Truth?

6. *Evaluate* the map by seeing how useful it is to others. Ultimately the test of any communication effort, including a map, is its effectiveness in conveying ideas. A map is useful if someone else can follow it. As part of the design loop, a map can be tested for its clarity, and redesigned if necessary.

This list is not exhaustive, but it should suggest some of the value of mapping in the curriculum. Each of these topics is developed in detail in Chapter 4, "Stories," which also looks more specifically at the relationship between graphs and maps.

The next section of this chapter will focus on how maps communicate and where they fit in the scheme of art, science, and technology. The final section looks at how children learn to map.

What is a map, really? Is a map more like a drawing or a photograph? Is it supposed to be a picture of the way a space really is, or is it someone's personal view of that space? Does mapping belong in art, science, technology, or all of the above?

Most maps are drawings. Like many drawings, maps use two-dimensional surfaces to represent real objects located elsewhere in physical space. But a map is not just another drawing; it is a special kind of drawing. We expect it to show the way things really are arranged in space. When we look at a drawing, we understand that it may or may not be telling the truth. Many drawings are impressionistic: They may tell us more about the artist than about his or her subject. But a map is different; it is supposed to show us what is really there, so we can "follow the map." In this sense, a map is more like a photograph than like a drawing.

But wait. Is even a photograph really an objective picture of things? A professional photographer captures the same scenery differently from a

tourist. The professional knows how to use lighting, composition, the type of film, and even the developing procedure to make the picture express a point of view. Could a map be any more objective than a photograph? Like both drawings and photographs, a map is designed to tell a story, to convey an idea, to make a point. In short, a map is a form of expressive communication. It offers the reader a picture of the territory, but not just any picture. It is a picture that has been fashioned from the viewpoint of the mapmaker.

This last statement may seem surprising. Some maps do appear to be completely accurate, detached, and objective views of the territory they claim to represent. Does every map selectively present only a particular point of view? A road map? A U.S. Government topographical map? Actually, yes. Look at any road map. Ask yourself, *What does this map show, what does it emphasize, and what does it leave out?*

Figue 2-1 shows a portion of the AAA map on "New York City and Vicinity." The map shows Manhattan in some detail. The other side of this map shows New York and New Jersey counties surrounding Manhattan and all the major approach roads. The full map of Manhattan identifies many hotels, convention facilities, over ten museums and libraries, many historic and landmark buildings, six colleges, five hospitals, two railroad stations, and several cultural centers.

Can this be considered an objective picture of Manhattan? Although most streets and highways in the region are shown, the subways and bus routes are not. This is a map designed for automobile drivers. A focus on public transportation, an ideal way to get around Manhattan once you are there, takes a different sort of map. Also missing on the full map is the top part of Manhattan, north from 168th Street. Although not a major destination for New York visitors, this area does include the Cloisters, the George Washington Bridge, and Columbia Presbyterian Hospital. Finally, those familiar with Lower Manhattan will note that many of the tiny streets that characterize the area are left out.

2-1: **New York City and Vicinity.** © AAA. *Used by permission.*

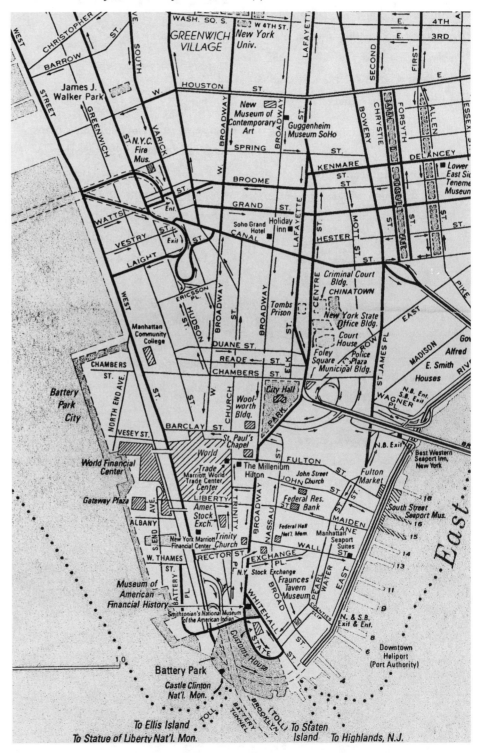

In an area filled with streets and landmark buildings, not all can be included. Map-making always involves trade-offs. The designers of the map in Figure 2-1 made decisions common to all map-makers:

- What is important to the users of our map?
- In order to provide lots of detail for an important destination, what do we have to leave out?
- How much detail can we include before it gets in the way of legibility?

Is this an "objective" map of Manhattan? It shows the Manhattan that many of us are interested in, but subway riders or those walking the tiny streets in the oldest part of the city would want a different map.

No map can show everything. Every map should be biased toward its intended user. It's up to the map-reader to figure out the bias of the map. The map key tells the kind of information provided in the map and, implicitly, the intended audience.

But Is It Art?

If a map is not a thorough, accurate representation, then what is it? Is a map a work of art? Many maps, including many professional maps, old and new, and many children's maps, certainly do have an artistic flair to them. But calling something a work of art would seem to require more than this. Art is the artist's personal expression about the nature of things. Because art is such a personal statement, you can't check it against reality in the same way you can test a scientific hypothesis. However, there are other ways to evaluate art. These are not our focus, because most maps are not intended primarily as works of art.

Maps as Tools for Science

Scientists, like artists, observe the world carefully to look for hidden patterns and relationships. However, the fundamental goals of science and art are different. Art calls for the widest possible variety of ways of looking at the world. Every work of art makes a personal statement, and there is no point in trying to reconcile them with each other. Science, in contrast, looks for unifying themes and principles. One goal of science is that all scientists arrive at a common understanding; another is that more and more phenomena be explained in terms of fewer and fewer basic concepts. Artists celebrate the diversity of personal and cultural world-views, while scientists pursue the quest for universal agreement and simplicity.

Maps play an important part in science education. Many if not most of the concepts of science are well illustrated by drawings and diagrams. Often as not, these show the relationships between things in space. A picture of a lever, which shows the relationship between fulcrum, effort, and load, is a kind of map. So is a circuit diagram or a sketch of the parts of a plant, not to mention a map of the solar system. These maps are not like photographs. Their purpose is not to show everything, but rather to present some of the underlying relationships, which form the conceptual framework of science. It is just as important to ask what they leave out as what they include.

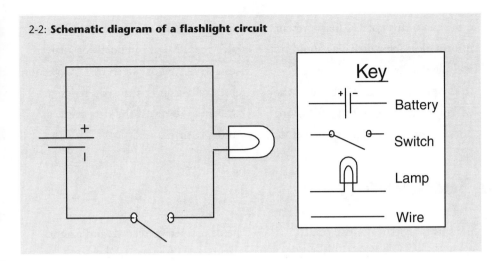

2-2: **Schematic diagram of a flashlight circuit**

For example, a circuit diagram like the one in Figure 2-2 shows the path of the current through the battery and bulb, but not the colors of the wires nor the exact shape of the components. These details are simply not relevant to the underlying principles of how the circuit works. They might be important to someone trying to build the circuit, but that requires a different kind of map. Similarly, a map of the solar system is likely to show the orbits of the planets (which would not appear in any photograph), but is less concerned with the exact position of the planets at any moment in time. These types of maps are tools for understanding.

Maps as Tools for Analysis

Children can also make their own maps as part of their science investigations. Children may map the temperature in different parts of the room, light and shadow on a window sill, types of plant and insect life in an abandoned lot, or drainage patterns on a hillside during a storm. In each case, mapping is a way of organizing data from a field study. Showing the data on a map reveals spatial relationships, suggests patterns and causal connections, and raises further questions that can be answered by further inquiry.

Figure 2-3 shows a temperature map of a large drafty classroom. The contours represent different temperatures.

This map raises a variety of questions about the drafts and heat sources in

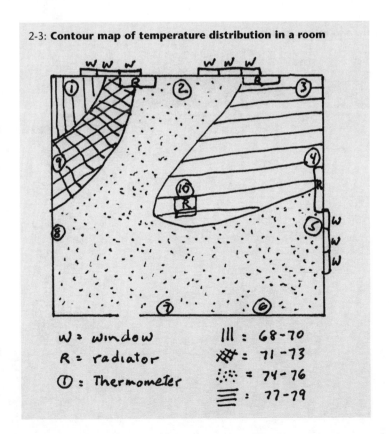

2-3: **Contour map of temperature distribution in a room**

W = window
R = radiator
① = Thermometer

||| : 68-70
XX : 71-73
∴ : 74-76
☰ : 77-79

the room. Where is the heat coming from? Where is it leaking out? Are any of the windows open or broken, or are they just old windows that don't keep the heat in very well? Used in this way, a map is a tool for analysis. Like any other map, this type of map presents information selectively. It should not include details that are irrelevant to the problem at hand, because they will only add clutter and confusion. For example, it would not be helpful to try to show too much furniture on this map. Maps intended for analysis can work well or not so well. A criterion for evaluation is: Can you redesign this map to reveal the data patterns more clearly?

Maps Are a Form of Technology

Science and technology are so closely related that they are often confused. Neither enterprise could proceed very far without the other. However, like science and art, their goals are different. The goal of science, as mentioned above, is to seek a common understanding of the way things are. Technology, on the other hand, seeks to change the way things are through human intervention. Technologies are invented by humans to extend their natural capabilities. For example, breathing is natural, and therefore not part of technology; breathing under water is possible only by virtue of SCUBA and other technologies. Similarly, writing is a technology that extends the human memory, enables communication over long distances, and offers a wealth of other possibilities.

Maps constitute a technology that helps us specify, record, and extend our knowledge of physical space. In addition, maps can be tools for the design or redesign of other technologies. This aspect of mapping is illustrated by an architect's floor plan, which is a tool used in the design of a building. In redesigning their classroom, children might make maps to show both the current arrangement and proposed alternatives, as in Figure 2-4.

2-4: **Classroom before and after redesign**

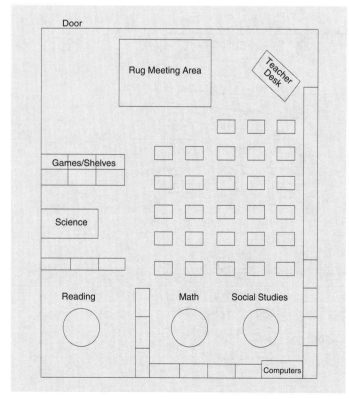
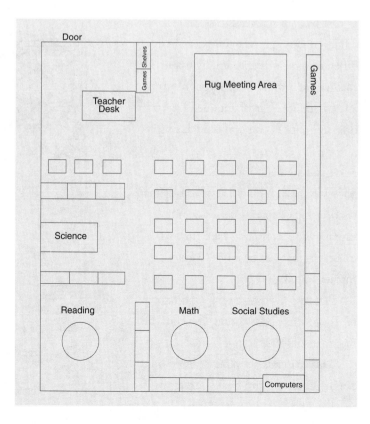

2-5: **A teacher's map of a folding chair**

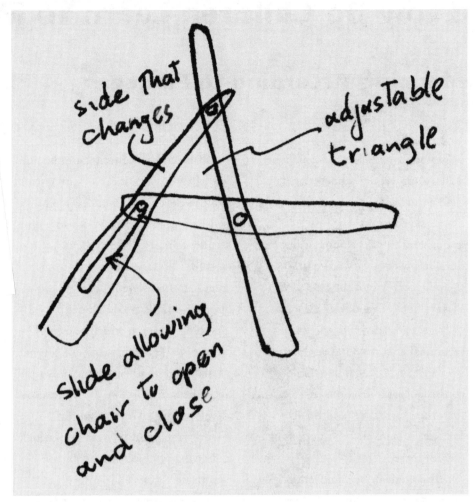

As children test and refine their own maps, they engage in what we call the mapping process, analogous to the writing process. Initial drafts of a map are refined on the basis of feedback from a map-reader:

- Is it clear what the map represents?
- Do the relationships in the map correspond to the relationships in the thing mapped?
- Can one follow the map?

Testing the map is essential, because it is the only point that the draft of the map is measured against the criteria it is supposed to meet. The possibility of testing against established criteria, and redesigning, are what make mapping a form of technology.

How Do Children Learn to Map?

Mapping According to Piaget

Mapping involves a development of skills, or procedural knowledge, rather than an increase in content knowledge. The basic concepts that help us understand this development in procedural knowledge vary according to the point of view of the researcher. Piaget's book, *The Child's Conception of Space,* is divided into three main sections that correspond to three major ways in which, Piaget says, children construct spatial relations: topological first, then projective, and finally Euclidean. Here are explanations of each of these.

Topological: Beginning around age two and continuing to around nine years old, children master such qualitative relations as nearness, separation, order, and being open or closed. In a child's drawing of the buildings on a block, an early stage has buildings drawn without concern for which is next to which. Topological development is revealed by drawing buildings next to each other that, in reality, are next to one another. Likewise, buildings separated from one another in reality are shown separated in the drawing. Finally, the buildings are in the same order in the drawing as on the street.

Projective: Beginning around the age of three years and continuing to around eleven, children develop a sense of projective space. This involves the development of perspective, the ability to understand how things appear from different points of view. Projective skills are developed by mapping games in which one child tries to duplicate the (unseen) construction of another, relying only upon the other's description. They are also developed by activities that say: Identify the point of view from which a drawing of objects on a tabletop was made.

Euclidean: Euclidean understandings develop from approximately four to fourteen years of age. These include the ability to handle coordinate systems, estimate distances, and interpret and produce maps to scale. Euclidean abilities are developed by activities in which children determine the location of a space on a grid through reference to its row and column.

A Current View:
Look to What Children Do, Not Piaget's Theory

If we accept the Piagetian view, we tend to limit the experiences we provide for children. Worse, we stop seeing what children are really capable of doing. Piaget's experimental approach to studying children's understanding of space used abstract tasks and unfamiliar surroundings. These are conditions in which children are least able to show the capacities they have developed. Moreover, Piaget didn't study children's understanding of maps, use of maps, or their map-making. The applications of Piaget's theories to mapping have all been by way of extrapolations. One of the results of Piagetian influence is that children are rarely asked to make maps before second or third grade or even later.

Over the past two decades researchers have begun to look more closely at young children and maps. Spencer, Blades, and Morsely (1989) report several studies, including their own, that show that 5- and 6-year-olds have already developed impressive mapping skills. They can look at an aerial photograph and identify several of its features. Aerial photos are similar to maps in that they are reduced in scale and require some abstraction since they present a view of things that children don't normally see.

Spencer and his colleagues set up a room with four boxes, each in the middle of a wall. They hid a toy in one of the boxes, indicating which one on a map of the room. Young children (four to six) were able to use the map to find the toy. This was easiest when the map was oriented in the same way as the room, but by the time children are six they are able to rotate the map through 90 or 180 degrees in order to use it correctly. Young children can also begin to use simple coordinate systems. Spencer and his colleagues found that 6-year-olds could locate objects on a four-by-four grid. One axis was labeled 1, 2, 3, and 4 and the other a, b, c, and d. Given the coordinates, such as 2c, the 6-year-old is able to find the object.

While Spencer et al. wrote of children's understanding of maps, Roger Downs (1985) wrote of their map-making. He also calls attention to our own tendency to judge maps in terms of "the Rand McNally view of the world." From the standard map perspective, maps are inferior if they incorporate multiple points of view, or if the size and spacing of objects lack proportionality. Downs reminds us that architectural plans use three views to represent a building adequately and that medieval paintings and maps regularly distorted size and spacing in order to call attention to what was of importance. In looking at children's maps, we should view them as attempts to present a child's own understanding of a space. We should expect to see a wide range of mapping skills displayed.

Matthews, four decades after Piaget, wrote *Making Sense of Place: Children's Understanding of Large-Scale Environments.* It incorporates the work of Downs, Spencer, and many others. He presents four basic concepts to describe the progression of a child's development: orientation, scale, coordinates, and symbols. You will see some overlap with the concepts Piaget uses to understand children's development. However Matthews, like Spencer, has a much broader understanding of what children are able to do. Matthews' four basic concepts are:

- **Orientation (Direction):** Orienting a map to a landscape. Knowledge of the convention that north is at the top. Deciding what viewpoint or perspective is taken.
- **Scale:** Initially this is an awareness of relative sizes. It develops into the ability to determine what scale to use and how to represent a landscape at a proportionately reduced size.

- **Coordinates (Location):** The ability to find locations by use of alpha-numeric coordinates.
- **Symbols:** The ability to select ways to represent various aspects of the landscape and to construct the representation.

Orientation

Have you ever looked at the floor plan of a store, usually mounted on a wall, with the hope of finding out where, for example, the linens are? A "You are here" arrow tells your present location. Now you have to figure out how the floor plan and arrow relate to you and the area you can see. This "figuring out" is orienting. If you are lucky, the area at the top of the floor plan lies directly ahead of you, the right side of the map shows areas to your right, and so forth. If you are unlucky, you will have to do a mental rotation of the floor plan through 90 or 180 degrees before it lines up with the real world. When you know the relation between the floor plan and the floor, you can use the plan to go to the place labeled "Linens."

A common way to orient a map (or floor plan or other form of map) to the real world is by landmarks. To use this method, you must be able to locate the landmark on your map as well as in the real world. Then turn the map until the direction from your location on the map to the landmark is the same as the direction from you to the landmark in the real world. With the map thus oriented, the direction of your destination on the map is the same as its direction in the real world.

Spencer and his colleagues modified the experiment where a toy was hidden in one of four boxes. They placed a landmark next to one of the boxes and on the map. When they hid the toy in the box next to the landmark, or furthest from it, children found the toy more easily, even when the map was not oriented with the room.

Scale

Children begin school with a basic, intuitive sense of scale. Many toys are scale models of the real thing, and most children's drawings represent real things at a much smaller scale. Every child is aware that his or her drawing of a tree is not the same size as a real tree, but has many of the same features at a reduced scale. The same is true of a toy car, a doll, an action figure, or a house made of blocks. Children make use of this intuitive feeling for scale when they read maps and when they begin to make their own.

Although they come to school with a basic awareness of scale, children nevertheless have tremendous difficulty in dealing with issues of relative size and scale in a systematic way. This difficulty is reflected in their early efforts to read scale maps and drawings. For example, children are unable to explain why two maps of the same territory but drawn to different scales show the same region differently. They will insist that one of the maps is "wrong." The region "really is" bigger than that.

More departures from accurate scale arise as children construct their own maps and drawings of the territory. A child draws his or her desk much larger than the others in the classroom; the TV is as large as the dresser it is sitting on; the child in the drawing is just as large as the tree she is standing next to; the hand has five fingers, but they are so big you can barely see the rest of the hand! There are a variety of issues at work in each of these examples, and developmental issues may or may not be at stake in each case. A minimum of instruction in drawing to scale, or even just a request that "if it's bigger than your desk, then it should look bigger than your desk on the map," may be sufficient to elicit a map drawn more closely to scale.

When a child draws his desk bigger than any of the others, he is probably making a statement about relative importance, not relative size. Also, the TV on the dresser may be intended more as a symbol than as a realistic drawing. A symbol need not be drawn to scale. In fact, it really cannot be because it "stands for" the object in a different way than a scale drawing. The person drawn the same size as the tree,

and the five fingers which dominate the hand, may reflect yet another problem not directly related to sense of scale. In a typical child's drawing, a tree has fewer features than a person, and the five fingers are the most intricate features of a hand. Simply fitting everything in may dictate that the fingers and the person have to be drawn relatively larger with respect to their surroundings.

Chapter 4, "Stories," describes some techniques for introducing children to scale mapping. In the course of these activities, children develop more than just an ability to make scale maps. They also address some basic math concepts such as ratio and proportion in the context of solving real problems: "How are we going to fit the whole cafeteria on this one sheet of paper?"

Coordinates

As with scale, children early on develop intuitive notions of how to specify locations on a four-by-four grid. Games such as "May I?" and "Simon Says," many board games, and dance routines involve such actions as "take one step forward," "move one step to your left," etc. In many cities, the

street layout is based on a more extensive coordinate system in which the streets themselves may even be numbered or lettered in sequence. A direction such as "Walk one block south, and then two blocks west" also reflects basic ideas about coordinates. Some basic thinking about coordinate grids is already a part of children's experiences. Young children may also have school experiences related to a coordinate system. A pre-K class we know plays "Turtle" on its way to the computer center when they are learning Logo: forward 10, left 90, forward 20, etc.

As with scale, however, these intuitive understandings may not translate into more systematic work. Asked to find a location from its coordinates, children may not be able to, although research reported by Mathews (1992) suggests that this skill develops at a remarkably early age between four and six years. In Chapters 3 and 4 of this book, you will learn about some mapping games that stimulate children to invent their own coordinate systems—for example, to identify locations on a hidden tic-tac-toe board.

2-6: **Child's drawing showing symbolic representation of real objects**

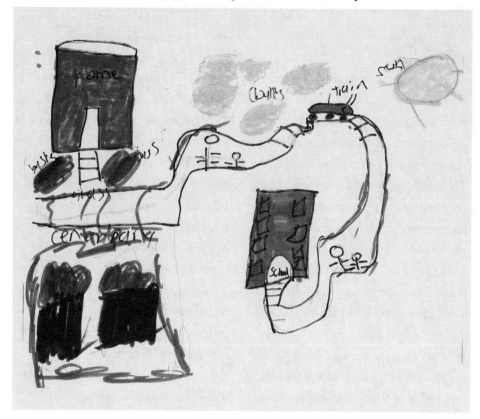

Symbols

Symbols are also very familiar to children. They quickly learn that red means "Stop" and green means "Go." They learn to read a huge variety of other symbols as well, ranging from the teacher raising two fingers to signal "Quiet" to the graphic symbol near the elevator that says "In case of fire, use the stairs." Even more important, but perhaps less obviously, they live in a world where corporate logos and other commercial symbols are pervasive. Long before they can read or write, children recognize McDonald's by the golden arches, Nike by the famous check sign, Coca Cola by the red letters, and many, many more.

Besides reading symbols, children also learn to write them, and much of children's early artwork is as much symbolic as realistic. For example, as shown in Figure 2-6, many children represent the sun by a circle with a face and rays. Similarly, buildings are shown as rectangles and train tracks as lines across a pair of parallel lines. These are not intended as realistic representations of the sun, of houses, or of tracks, but rather as conventional symbols or icons.

Although children are immersed in a world of symbols, they may have little conscious awareness of what symbols are and how they function. Looking at a map, for example, a child may misinterpret completely what the symbols are intended to mean. Matthews (1992) cites the example of a study in which children were asked to explain the significance of an airplane icon, which was intended to represent an airport. Many children believed that it represented a single airplane, and that if the plane flew away, the symbol should be removed from the map!

Unless taught to do so explicitly, children may also have difficulty in using symbols on their own maps. Chapter 4 cites an example of a child who constructed an elaborate key on her map, but then failed to use any of the symbols on the key in the map itself. More often, children use symbols inconsistently, applying them in some instances but not others. With some instruction, children can begin to see the use of symbols as a way to reduce clutter and make their maps more readable.

Chapter 3
ACTIVITIES

Getting Started With Mapping

Often, the most difficult step in introducing a new topic into your curriculum is figuring out how to get started. This guide provides many entry points into the world of mapping.

Scavenger Hunts, Brainstorming, and **Discussion** are three strategies that support participants' initial explorations of maps and mapping. They are suggested throughout this curriculum as vehicles for getting students to start thinking about the objects, concepts, ideas, and skills that connect technology to their everyday lives. These three strategies introduce the collection of activities, methods, and approaches that practitioners who have worked with mapping have used as entry points.

Scavenger Hunts

Scavenger hunts are searches in both likely and unlikely places for items, objects, materials, information, and ideas relevant to mapping. Engaging in a scavenger hunt is a way of collecting information (data). A scavenger hunt is an excellent starting activity for any age of learner. As students collect examples in the world around them, they use science inquiry skills (e.g., observation, data collection) needed for mapping and begin to focus on a particular question such as, "What is a map?"

Brainstorming

Brainstorming is a mental scavenger hunt. It encourages participants to freely express their ideas and notions about a topic in order to develop an idea of the range of things that might be included in the topic.

A preliminary brainstorming session may precede a scavenger hunt or be incorporated as part of the sharing of things collected as a result of a scavenger hunt. When working with students around mapping and design, brainstorming often gives the teacher a good sense of where learners are on understanding maps and mapping.

To support students in spontaneously proposing ideas and/or solutions, certain ground rules need to be established and roles designated for brainstorming:

- There must be a recorder, someone who writes down all responses.
- Accept and record all responses without censorship.
- Do not allow discussion or evaluation until brainstorming is over.
- As facilitator, ask for clarification/ elaboration when necessary and when no one else in the group does.
- Sometimes a participant repeats a response that has already been made. Redirect that participant; encourage the participant to come up with her own idea.

Discussion

Discussion is fundamental to the teaching and learning process. It is often the most immediate way to get feedback. Strategies for effective classroom discussions around mapping topics include:

- Identifying goals of the discussion
- Developing effective questioning techniques, such as:
  - Developing focusing questions in advance of the discussion
  - Rephrasing your questions if the originals prove to be unclear
  - Perfecting probing skills to help students clarify and elaborate on their concepts and ideas
- Developing good listening skills
- Establishing an atmosphere that encourages participation from all learners

Although discussion is critical in getting started, it permeates all aspects of the process. Learning to use this strategy effectively early on will benefit all aspects of the teaching/learning process in your classroom.

Overview of Mapping Activities

Mapping offers an edited collection of activities developed with our collaborating teachers. The collection is extensive but by no means exhaustive. We encourage you to think of your own activities. The activities are grouped in five sections:

- Pre-Mapping and Supporting Mapping Activities
- Defining and Interpreting Maps
- Starting to Make Maps
- An Upper Elementary Sequence
- A Middle School Sequence

"Pre-Mapping and Supporting Mapping Activities" emphasize observational and communication skills. "Defining and Interpreting Maps" activities are those that introduce children to the broad range of maps and of information they can obtain from them. These activities also give teachers a window into children's varied conceptions and differential knowledge of maps. "Starting to Make Maps" provides activities used by teachers throughout the elementary grades to start children in the process of representing the three dimensional world in the two dimensions of a sheet of paper.

Once you have gotten yourself and your students started with mapping, it is helpful to have a sense of how others have proceeded. "An Upper Elementary Sequence" presents work done by Felice Piggott with fifth graders. She uses mapping as a theme that integrates science/technology with English language arts, mathematics, social studies, and art. "A Middle School Sequence" presents Michael Gatton's work, which is in the context of a middle school science class. Felice's and Michael's stories of this work are included in Chapter 4, "Stories."

All of the activities are correlated to standards in Science, Mathematics, and English Language Arts, and several to standards in Social Studies. The relevant standards are referenced in abbreviated form for each activity. The full standards references appear at the end of this chapter.

ACTIVITIES AT A GLANCE

Level	Activity Title	Page	Purpose
Pre-Mapping & Supporting Mapping	#1: Observing a Box: Top and Side Views	37	To recognize and distinguish between different points of view
	#2: Shapes from a Bird's-Eye View	38	To begin mapping using a small, familiar space to record surface shapes
	#3: Map Your Hand	41	To begin an exploration of mapping
	#4: Large-Group Mapping Games	43	To develop skills in observation, identifying things, describing locations, following directions, and orienting oneself in a physical space
	#5: Small-Group Mapping Games	45	To develop skills in observation, identifying things, describing locations, following directions, and orienting oneself
Defining and Interpreting Maps	#6: Brainstorming: What Is a Map?	50	To gain the understanding that maps are more than flat pieces of paper and are used in a variety of places and for different purposes
	#7: Map Scavenger Hunt: What Is a Map?	51	To gain the understanding that maps are more than flat pieces of paper and are used in a variety of places and for different purposes
	#8: Analysis: What Is a Map?	52	To begin to develop criteria for what constitutes a map
	#9: What Maps Say	54	To use a simple map to get information about a classroom area
Starting to Make Maps	#10: Drawing Desktops	55	To explore perspective and point of view while graphically representing spatial relations among objects
	#11: Map Your Room	56	To get started with mapping by mapping a familiar space, then analyzing ways to represent objects and spaces
	#12: Find North	58	To explore tools and techniques for locating, identifying, and using cardinal directions
	#13: The Smartest Gerbils	60	To determine students' understanding of maps and their ability to make maps
	#14: Desk Maps	62	To create maps that communicate clearly and test them
	#15: Brainstorming: What Can We Map?	64	To get students to think of other kinds of maps beyond road, state, and country maps
An Upper Elementary Sequence	#16: The Route to School	66	To develop skills in making and evaluating route maps: symbols, landmarks, and orientating devices in maps of large-scale areas
	#17: Route to a Destination Within the Classroom	68	To further develop skills in making and evaluating route maps
	#18: Mapping with a Master Map: Establishing Scale	70	To develop understanding of scale (what scale is, which scale is appropriate)
	#19: Placing Desks on a Master Map	72	To practive drawing features on a map to scale
A Middle School Sequence	#20: Locating Ourselves in Space	74	To use two points along adjacent walls to determine a location in the classroom
	#21: Mapping a Classroom	76	To map a space that will later be used to collect data on diffusion
	#22: Mapping Diffusion in a Petri Dish	78	To apply mapping techniques to describe the process of diffusion through a liquid
	#23: Mapping Diffusion of Gas in the Classroom	81	To use mapping techniques to visually represent an invisible process

Activity №1

Observing a Box: Top and Side Views

Grade Level
Early childhood

Purpose
To recognize and distinguish between different points of view

Overview
This activity taps into young students' observation skills by having them focus on a single object and talk about what they see by describing the relationships between parts of the object and the whole from different points of view.

Concepts
- An object looks different—has different shapes—from different perspectives.
- The same part of an object looks different from different perspectives.

Skills
- Observing
- Comparing observations
- Recording observations

Standards
Benchmarks for Science Literacy: #1B

Standards for the English Language Arts: #4

Principles and Standards for School Mathematics: Com2

National Science Education Standards: A

Time Needed
45 minutes

Materials
For each group, a box with writing and symbols on the top and sides, such as a crayon box or chalk box.

Procedure
A. Getting Started
1. You may wish to talk with the children about other work they have done in observing things. Explain that today they are going to look very closely at just one thing and notice how what they can see changes as their position changes.
2. Divide the class into small groups. Place a crayon box in the middle of each group of desks.

B. Top View
1. Have each group stand in a circle around their desks so they can look down on the box of crayons.

2. Ask children at different parts of the circle to describe what they see on the top of the box. Ask children in corresponding positions in other groups what they see. Make sure the differences in perspective come out.
3. Rotate children around the box so they see how the box looks from another perspective. Talk about the different observations.

C. Side View
1. With children seated, ask them to describe what has changed as they look at the box.
2. Then ask the children to put their chins on the desk. Again let them tell what they see.
3. Rotate children around the box so they see how another side looks. Talk about the different observations.
4. Ask children to describe how the appearance of the box changes as they look at it from different sides. Then ask them to compare how the box looks when they can see the top with how it looks when they can't see the top.

Activity № 2

Shapes from a Bird's-Eye View

Grade Level
1 and up; all experiential levels

Purpose
To begin mapping using a small, familiar space to record surface shapes

Overview
This basic activity focuses students on observing the arrangement of objects. Students search for, recognize, identify, and record surface shapes from a "bird's-eye view." The end result is a map of a small, manageable space.

Concepts
The map of an area should contain the same objects as the area you are mapping.

Skills
- Observing objects and their spatial relationships
- Drawing objects in the same spatial relationships to each other as they have in the classroom

Standards
Benchmarks for Science Literacy: #1B, #2C

Standards for the English Language Arts: #12

Principles and Standards for School Mathematics: Com2, G1, G2

National Science Education Standards: A

Time Needed
1 class period

Materials
For demonstration:
- Objects with square, triangular, round, and rectangular top surfaces (building blocks work well)
- Chart paper
- Marker
- Masking tape

For each group:
- Four blocks of different shapes
- Pencils
- Paper
- Worksheet #2 ("Classroom Shapes")

Procedure
A. Whole Class

1. Arrange six to ten blocks of different sizes and colors in an area on the floor. Enclose the arrangement using masking tape or something comparable to define a rectangular boundary. Draw a comparable rectangle on the board.

2. Ask students to stand around the rectangular boundary. Tell them, "Pretend you are a bird. Look down on the rectangle and name the shapes you see."

3. Ask a student to point to any one of the blocks on the floor. Ask that student, "What shape is it?" Students might respond by assigning the name of the three-dimensional object. Explain that you want them to look only at the top surface.

4. Direct students to the rectangle drawn on the board. Explain that you want them to represent the floor object on the board by drawing its shape. Ask a student to tell you where on the rectangle (map) to draw the shape. Using markers that correspond to colors of the blocks/boxes, draw the shape in the proper location so

students can see that the map on the board is related to the rectangle and the collection of blocks/boxes on the floor. Repeat, until the entire arrangement has been drawn on the board map.

B. Group work

1. Distribute four blocks of different shapes, pencils, and two pieces of paper to each student's desk. Tell the children that they will arrange the four blocks on a piece of paper, then use the other piece of paper to make a map of where the blocks are. Explain that they shouldn't move the blocks once they have begun to draw them!

2. Circulate around the room to see how each child is doing. Where a representation is inaccurate, ask questions to lead the child to see the spatial relationships between blocks and between a block and the sides of the paper it sits on.

3. Bring the class together briefly to share their maps and talk about what helped them know where they should draw each object.

C. Finding More Shapes

1. Distribute copies of Worksheet #2 (Classroom Shapes, p. 40). Challenge students to find at least five different shapes in the classroom and to record their finds on the worksheet. (If students find more than five, they can record them on an additional worksheet.) Continue to remind students that when they are looking down at objects on the floor, they have a bird's-eye view. Objects on the walls are viewed straight on, horizontally.

2. Ask students to share the shapes they have found and where they found them. You might want students to begin by naming shapes that they know and by recording the identified shapes on the board.

3. Ask students to compare shapes that were found on the most objects and shapes that were found on the fewest objects.

Worksheet #2

Classroom Shapes

Name/Group _____

Date _____

Below are five columns. At the top of each column draw a shape. Below each shape, list all the things you can find in the classroom that have the same shape.

Which shape has the most objects under it? _____

Which shape has the fewest objects under it? _____

How did you start making your lists? _____

_____

Activity № 3

Map Your Hand

Grade Level
K-3, with no prior experience necessary

Purpose
To begin an exploration of mapping

Overview
This activity taps into the appeal of a classic early childhood activity and is an ideal entry point into mapping for less experienced learners. Through this activity children focus on observing and recording a familiar part of themselves as a way to begin exploring mapping.

Concepts
One-to-one correspondences: the lines on the map of the hand are in the same positions as the lines on your hand.

Skills
• Observing
• Recording
• Comparing the recorded observation to the thing observed

Standards
Benchmarks for Science Literacy: #1B, #2C

Standards for the English Language Arts: #12

Principles and Standards for School Mathematics: G2

National Science Education Standards: A

Time Needed
2 class sessions

Materials
• Pencil
• Paper
• Colored pencil
• Worksheet #3

Procedure
A. Getting Started (1 period)

1. Ask students to describe what is the same about all people and what is different.

2. Ask students to take a good look at the palms of their hands and tell what they see.

3. Ask the students to draw the outline of one of their hands, palm up.

4. Then ask students to look closely at the lines in the palm of their hand and then add those lines to the palm in their drawing.

5. When students have finished their drawings, have them compare their drawings and talk about what they have in common and how they are different.

Note: With young children, this unit may end with posting the hand maps on the wall.

B. Sharpening Observations (1 period, 2nd and 3rd graders)

1. Ask children how they could be sure that a drawing of a hand is accurate. Record their ideas on chart paper. Among the strategies are:

   • Comparing the number of big lines on the palm that are on the actual hand and on the map.

   • Comparing where the lines of the palm are located on the actual hand and on the map. For example...

     • Does a line begin close to the base of a finger? If so, which finger?
     • Where does the line end?
     • How long is the line?
     • Does it cross other big lines?

2. Distribute Worksheet #3. Tell the children that their palm map is a "first draft" drawing. Now they will use the "Edit the Map of Your Hand" worksheet to revise and improve their maps.

3. After students have finished editing their hand maps, discuss the changes they made and why they made them.

4. Post the edited hand maps around the room.

Worksheet #3

Edit the Map of Your Hand

Name/Group   Date
_____

Follow the steps below to compare your hand to the map of your hand. When you make changes to your map, don't erase anything. Instead, use a different color to edit your map. This will be your editing color. Using a different color and keeping the old lines makes it easy for you to show others how you have improved the map of your hand.

1. Check the Size and Shape

   • Place your hand on the map of your hand, palm up.

   • Is the map of your hand the same size as your hand?   [ ] Yes   [ ] No

   • Is the map of your hand the same shape as your hand?   [ ] Yes   [ ] No

   • Make any needed corrections to the outline of your hand using your editing color.

2. Add Missing Lines

   • Look at the big lines on your palm. How many big lines do you have? _____

   • Look at the map of your hand. How many big lines did you draw? _____

   • If any lines are missing, draw them in with your editing color.

3. Check the Placement of the Lines

   • Find the biggest line on your hand. Where does the line begin? Is it near the side of the hand? Is it near the base of a finger? Make a dot in the same place on your hand map.

   • Where does the biggest line end? Make a dot on the map where the line ends.

   • Are these points the beginning and end of that line on your hand map? If not, improve your map by drawing in the correct line. Use the editing color.

   • Pick another line on your hand and go through the same steps. This is the way you make sure each line is accurate.

   • Check your hand to see if any big lines cross. Compare your map to see if the same lines cross at the same place. Correct them if they don't.

Activity № 4

Large-Group Mapping Games

Grade Level
2 and up

Purpose
To develop skills in observation, identifying things, describing locations, following directions, and orienting oneself in a physical space

Overview
The whole-class games described here give students the opportunity to use the class environment or large classroom maps to develop their skills in using directions to find things.

Concepts
Object locations can be described by cardinal directions, distances, and landmarks.

Skills
- Applying and integrating strategies for locating objects and places in physical space
- Observing spatial relationships
- Identifying and describing directions and spatial relationships
- Following directions

Standards
Benchmarks for Science Literacy: #1B

Standards for the English Language Arts: #12

Principles and Standards for School Mathematics: PS3

National Science Education Standards: A

Time Needed
1 class period

Materials
- Large map of the United States, or similar large map
- Signs: "North," "South," "East," "West"

Tip
These games require the ability to think and communicate in terms of directions. A good warm-up activity is "Simon Says," emphasizing use of right and left, up and down, east and west. For example, "Simon says, Face north," "Simon says, Lift the hand on your east side," "Simon says, Face north and then turn to your right."

Procedure
A. Classroom Places

1. Place the "North," "South," "East," "West" signs on the appropriate walls in the classroom. If necessary, review with the class what these signs mean.

2. Choose an object that is always present in the classroom: a shelf, a sign or picture on the wall, a particular window, the chalkboard, the fish tank, a rug, etc. This is the object whose location students will be trying to identify in this game.

3. Explain to the class that you are thinking of something that is in a particular place in the classroom. Their job is to figure out what it is by asking you questions that will help them figure out where it is. They can only ask you questions that can be answered with "Yes" or "No" and that are about the location of the object. Give one or two examples of acceptable and unacceptable questions— e.g., "Is it in the reading area?" (acceptable), "Is it on the west side of the room?" (acceptable), "Which side of the room is it on?" (unacceptable because it cannot be answered with "Yes" or "No"), or "Is it green?" (unacceptable because it is not about the location of the object). Establish the number of questions that can be asked—e.g., the game ends when either the object has been identified or students have asked 12 questions without identifying the object.

4. Have students raise their hands to ask questions. If a question can't be answered with "Yes" or "No," or does not refer to location, help the student rephrase it.

5. When students get the hang of the game, let them take turns being the person who chooses an object and answers questions.

B. Twenty Questions on a Map

This game is similar to "Classroom Places" except that the objective is to identify a place on a map rather than an object in a specific place in the classroom. Again the questions must be phrased so they can be answered by "Yes" or "No."

C. Follow-up Discussion

After either of these games, discuss the strategies that helped students identify a particular location. Record effective strategies on chart paper for future reference. Help students discover how a question that eliminates a large portion of the space or many possible locations is better than a question that eliminates only a small space or a single location. For example, "Is it a river?" either includes or excludes all rivers on a map, while "Is it the Mississippi River?" might eliminate only one of many possible locations or features on a map. However, "Is it the Mississippi River?" might be an effective question if it is already known that the feature is a river and its general location includes the area of the Mississippi.

Activity № 5

Small-Group Mapping Games

Grade Level
2 and up; all experiential levels

Purpose
To develop skills in observation, identifying things, describing locations, following directions, and orienting oneself.

Overview
"Mapping Games" is a set of 39 activity cards produced by the Elementary Science Study and published by Webster Division, McGraw-Hill Book Co., 1971. Teachers have found them useful as pre- and supporting activities for mapping. They provide opportunities for students to "play" with the tools of oral communication to convey information about spatial arrangements, which is one of the goals of the mapping process. The games in this activity are based on five of those cards.

Concepts
• Specific directions (e.g, "touching the right side of the orange square") are necessary. Ambiguous directions lead to errors.

• Grids of rows and columns, and orienting devices such as compasses (to the southeast) or clocks (in the direction of 5) give clarity and specificity to communication about location.

Skills
Using and following spatial directions (above, below, to the right, on top of, parallel to)

Standards
Benchmarks for Science Literacy: #1B, #2C

Standards for the English Language Arts: #12

Principles and Standards for School Mathematics: PS2, PS3, Com2, C3, G2

National Science Education Standards: A

Time Needed
1 class period to introduce games; students' free time thereafter

Materials
• Task cards for mapping games (Duplicate pages 47-49)
• Pencils
• Markers
• Cardboard divider

Procedure
A. Set-Up
1. Copy the Task Cards on pp. 47-49 for use with each game. Set up the following areas in the room: "Duplicating Tangram Problems," "Comparing Block Patterns," "Matching Geoboard Paths," "Blind Tic-Tac-Toe," and "Blind Checkers."

2. Set up a table with materials necessary for each game.

3. Demonstrate "Blind Tic-Tac-Toe" to give students a general idea of the games. Students then go on to play one of the games for themselves, followed by a discussion. Games are then available for use during free time.

B. Introduction to "Blind Tic-Tac-Toe"
1. Ask the children "Who knows how to play 'Tic-Tac-Toe?'" Have two volunteers come to the board to demonstrate how "Tic-Tac-Toe" is played.

2. After everyone is clear about the game, tell the class that you are going to change the game to make it harder: the two players will describe where they place their own marks, but they will be unable to see each other's tic-tac-toe grid.

3. Invite two more students to play this "Blind Tic-Tac-Toe." Have them sit at a table with a barrier (cardboard divider) between them.

4. Each student draws a tic-tac-toe grid. Assign one student to "X's" and one to "O's". The first draws an "X" on his grid and uses words to tell the other where to put this "X." If necessary, write down the instructions for yourself so you can repeat them word-for-word.

5. Before the two students continue, tell the rest of the students to make a "Tic-Tac-Toe" grid. Repeat the first player's instructions, word-for-word, as to where to place the first "X," and have all students place an "X" according to the way they understand the directions. Point out that they may not ask for clarification. If they're not sure about where to place the "X," they should do the best they can and continue with the game.

6. Resume the game, with the second player placing an "O" on her grid. She then uses words to tell the other player where to place an "O" on his grid. Continue in this way, with all students following the spoken instructions to the conclusion of the game.

7. When the game is over, give students a chance to compare their grids with one another. Have a discussion about problems students had understanding the directions. Encourage them to give examples of directions that were clear as well as those they had difficulty understanding. Point out that the purpose of the game is to use words to communicate as clearly as possible about locations on the grid.

C. Introduction to the Other Games

1. Introduce the available mapping games: "Duplicating Tangram Problems," "Comparing Block Patterns," "Matching Geoboard Paths," "Blind Tic-Tac-Toe," and "Blind Checkers."

2. Show students the materials needed for each game, including an instruction card.

3. Explain that each game is played in a way similar to "Blind Tic-Tac-Toe." In each game two students are separated by a cardboard divider that prevents them from seeing what the other is doing. One partner follows the other partner's instructions. The goal is for both partners to end up with the same arrangement. Two pairs of students are to be at each game. One pair observes while the other pair plays. Then they switch places.

4. Have the students select the game they want to play, go to the table for that particular game, and play the game.

5. In this first session, allow enough time so that students can really get involved. You might want to keep your instructions to a minimum. Students will be freer to experiment with activities and learn through trial and error.

D. Discussion

Ask students to share their experiences playing the games. Have them discuss the strategies they used to get better at each game.

Strategies/Tips

- Encourage students to maintain a record of their guesses, trials, and designs.

- Ask students to write their reflections on these mapping games, focusing on what they are learning about giving clear directions and about listening.

Activity №5

Task Cards for Mapping Games

Duplicating Block Patterns

Materials:
Pattern blocks (or other blocks) and a cardboard screen.

Directions:
- Each player takes a similar group of pattern blocks.
- Place the screen between the players so you cannot see what the other does.
- The first player makes a figure with the pattern blocks, then gives the other player instructions on how to build it.
- Following instructions, the second builds the figure.
- When the second figure is completed, remove the screen and compare the two. Are there any differences? How did they happen?
- If there are observers, ask them why the differences occurred.

Comparing Tangram Patterns

Materials:
Tangram pieces and a cardboard screen

Directions:
- Each player takes a similar group of tangram pieces.
- Place the screen between the players so you cannot see what the other does.
- The first player makes a figure with the tangram pieces, then gives the other player instructions on how to build it.
- Following instructions, the second builds the figure.
- When the second figure is completed, remove the screen and compare the two. Are there any differences? How did they happen?
- If there are observers, ask them why the differences occurred.

Matching Geoboard Paths

Materials:
Two geoboards, rubber bands or string, and a cardboard screen

Directions:
- Each player takes a geoboard and rubber bands or string.
- Place the screen between the players so you cannot see what the other does.
- The first player makes a figure on the geoboard using rubber bands or string to go from post to post.
- The first player then gives the other player instructions on how to make a similar figure.
- Following instructions, the second builds the figure.
- When the second figure is completed, remove the screen and compare the two. Are there any differences? How did they happen?
- If there are observers, ask them why the differences occurred.

Blind Tic-Tac-Toe

Materials:
Paper and pencil and a cardboard screen

Directions:
- Each player takes a pencil and sheet of paper and makes a tic-tac-toe grid.
- Place the screen between the players so you cannot see what the other does.
- The first player places an "X" in one of the tic-tac-toe cells and tells the second player where to place the "X."
- The second player writes in the "X," then places an "O" in one of the tic-tac-toe cells and tells the first player where to place the "O."
- Play continues back and forth until one wins the game, or it ends in a tie.
- When the game is completed, remove the screen and compare the two tic-tac-toe grids. Are there any differences? How did they happen?
- If the grids do not agree, do not count the game as a win for either player.
- If there are observers, ask them why the differences occurred.

Blind Checkers

Materials:
Two checkerboards and two sets of checkers

Directions:
- Each player takes a checkerboard and set of checkers, both black and red pieces.

- Each player sets up the pieces on both sides of the board. The players select their colors. Each player will play his or her own pieces, and move the opponent's pieces as directed to do.

- Place the screen between the players so you cannot see what the other does.

- Choose who goes first. In these directions, player one has the black pieces.

- The first player moves a black checker and tells the second player where to move the black checker on the second board.

- The second player now moves a red checker and tells player one where to move the red checker on player one's board.

- Play continues back and forth. Each player moves his or her own pieces, and moves the opponent's pieces according to instructions.

- When the game is completed, remove the screen and compare the two boards. Are there any differences? How did they happen?

- If there are observers, ask them why the differences occurred.

Note: This is difficult. There may be such confusion before the game is over that you have to stop and figure out where you went wrong. After you figure it out, start over.

Activity № 6

Brainstorming: What Is a Map?

Grade Level
2 and up; all experiential levels

Purpose
To gain the understanding that maps are more than flat pieces of paper and are used in a variety of places and for different purposes

Overview
This brainstorming activity encourages students to express their concepts and ideas spontaneously. To determine students' initial notions of what maps are (possibly before you send them off on a Scavenger Hunt), you might want to consider this preliminary activity. Brainstorming and scavenger hunts may be used as alternative or complementary ways to begin work on mapping.

Concepts
There are many ways to represent things graphically, including many different kinds of maps.

Skills
Listening and sharing ideas

Standards
Benchmarks for Science Literacy: #1B

Standards for the English Language Arts: #12

National Science Education Standards: A

Time Needed
15 minutes to an hour

Materials
- Chart paper
- Markers

Procedure
1. Gather the class in your regular meeting area to brainstorm "What is a map?" Remind students of the brainstorming rules and roles. If this is students' first time brainstorming, establish the rules and roles. (See page 34.)

2. Ask for volunteers to share with the group what they think a map is. Use questions like these to initiate discussion and keep it going:

   - What do you think of when you hear the word "map?"

   - How would you define a map?

   - What is a map?

   - What are maps used for?

   - Can you think of some different kinds of maps?

3. List all examples on chart paper.

4. When you are satisfied with the scope of students' responses, ask students to look at the list and point out anything they disagree with, are unsure of, or have specific questions about.

Strategies/Tips
Keep the session short and lively to maintain the interest of students.

Homework
Have all students bring in examples of maps for the following day. This is the first step for the Scavenger Hunt in Activity #7. Students should (with permission!) bring in as many examples of different kinds of maps as they can find. Encourage students to bring in examples of maps that raised questions during the brainstorming session.

Activity №7

*M*ap Scavenger Hunt: What Is a Map?

Grade Level
2 and up; all experiential levels

Purpose
To gain the understanding that maps are more than flat pieces of paper and are used in a variety of places and for different purposes

Overview
This activity uses the maps students bring in from the preceding homework assignment. It is an opportunity for students to compare and contrast, sort, count, and discuss the examples they have gathered in order to develop a preliminary understanding of what maps are and are not.

Concepts
There are many ways to represent things graphically, including many different kinds of maps.

Skills
Listening and sharing ideas; categorizing maps

Standards
Benchmarks for Science Literacy: #1B

Standards for the English Language Arts: #12

National Science Education Standards: A

Time Needed
15 minutes to 1 hour

Materials
• Student-collected maps

• Chart paper

• Pens

Procedure
Note: If your class had a full brainstorming session on "What Is a Map?", then you may want to keep this short, or combine it with the following activity, "Analyzing Maps."

1. Remind everyone that this is like a brainstorming session, so the same rules apply. (See page 34.)

2. Ask for volunteers to share with the group the maps they have found.

3. List all of the items on chart paper. Allow time for discussion of the items students have found, using questions like these:

• Why do you think this is a map?

• What is it a map of?

• How would someone use this map?

4. After the discussion, have students scrutinize the list of maps and make note of items that they believe may not fit into the category of maps. Record all responses along with the list of maps and keep it available for students to refer to in the future.

Tips/Strategies
Language and naming play a crucial role in the listing of examples. Students will have had to come up with a name for each item they are contributing to the list. These names/identifiers will be subject to discussion with the rest of the group.

Activity № 8

Analysis: What Is a Map?

Grade Level
2 and up; all experiential levels

Purpose
To begin to develop criteria for what constitutes a map

Overview
Students need to have a variety of ways to talk about their notions of maps and mapping. Once a list of brainstorming ideas or scavenger hunt examples has been compiled, students can begin to examine items on the list.

Concepts
Criteria can guide categorizing.

Skills
Recognizing similarities and differences

Standards
Benchmarks for Science Literacy: #1B

Standards for the English Language Arts: #12

Principles and Standards for School Mathematics: Com1, PS2, R1

National Science Education Standards: A

Time Needed
1 class period

Materials
• Brainstorming list from Activity #6 and/or scavenger hunt list from Activity #7

• Worksheet #8 (one for each student)

Procedure
1. Review the brainstorming and/or scavenger hunt lists as well as the questions raised about which items are really maps.

2. Distribute copies of Worksheet #8, "Analyzing Maps." Go over the worksheet to make sure everyone understands how to fill it out.

3. Divide the class into groups of four.

4. Have students work in their groups to fill out the worksheet. Each student should fill out a worksheet, but group members should discuss and agree on each item.

5. After groups have finished the worksheet, bring the class together and have each group report on its findings.

6. Help children identify and discuss differences in the lists, criteria, and sorting rules. Which rules seem to work best, and why?

Strategies/Tips
Sometimes it is difficult to determine whether an item is or is not a map. As students engage in additional mapping tasks and experiences, their notions of what a map is will change. As you and your students develop a clearer definition of "map," what belongs on a list of "maps" will become clearer. However, debates about what to count as a map may still arise. Enjoy and exploit these controversies as learning experiences.

Worksheet #8

nalyzing Maps

Name/Group _____   Date _____

1. Place each item on the Brainstorming and/or Scavenger Hunt lists in one of these three categories:

Maps	**Not Maps**	**Uncertain**

2. Discuss these questions with your group, and write the group's responses:

What do the things in the "Maps" column have in common? _____

_____

What do the things in the "Not Maps" column have in common? _____

_____

What prevents the "Not Maps" from being "Maps"? _____

_____

Make a rule for sorting things into "Maps" and "Not Maps." _____

_____

Use this rule on items in the "Uncertain" to decide if they are "Maps" or "Not Maps."

These are maps: _____

These are not maps: _____

Activity № 9

What Maps Say

Grade Level
1 and up; all experiential levels

Purpose
To get students started with mapping by investigating whether they can use a simple map (instead of going to the actual area) to find things and get information about an area

Overview
You can use this activity to help get a sense of students' ability to get information from a map. It helps assess to what extent students can use a map to identify where things are in the real world.

Concepts
Maps can be used to find out things that are in the area mapped.

Skills
• Observation

• Identifying and understanding symbols

Standards
Benchmarks for Science Literacy: #1B

Standards for the English Language Arts: #12

Principles and Standards for School Mathematics: Com1, Com2, G1, G2

National Science Education Standards: A

Time Needed
30 minutes to 1 hour, depending on age, grade, and experiential levels

Materials
A collection of different maps including two teacher-made maps: one of an area in the classroom where things students find interesting are kept and one of the teacher's desk

Procedure
1. Show the class a few samples of maps from your collection, including the two made by you. Explain that these are maps without going into any detail about what kind they are or the definition of "map."

2. Ask students to look at the maps and tell you what they see. Encourage them to talk about what they see by asking questions like these:

   • What does this map show?

   • Where is this in our classroom?

   • How many books are on the desk?

   • Where is one object in relation to another? (Use items from the maps.)

   • Is there a stapler on the desk?

   • What else is on the desk?

If students have difficulty with the concept that maps represent things in the area mapped, take an additional object, place it on the teacher's desk, and asked how you should change the map of the desk.

3. Call attention to the legend or key of a printed map and ask what it is and what it is for. Let children point out symbols in the key and where they are used on the map.

4. Explain to students that they can look for keys and symbols on other maps they might see or use in the future.

Extensions
• Encourage students to examine the different maps from your map collection, identify the symbols, and figure out what they stand for.

• When you go on a field trip, obtain maps of the roads from the school to the destination and make copies, including a copy of the key. Discuss how you might get to the destination, then take the maps on the trip to see how you actually go.

• When you go on a field trip, obtain maps of the destination, if available. Museums and zoos usually have these. They can be used to plan what you will see and how you will find those things or places.

Activity № 10

Drawing Desktops

Grade Level
1 and up

Purpose
To explore perspective and point of view while graphically representing spatial relations among objects

Overview
This is an upper grade variation of Activity #2, "Shapes from a Bird's-Eye View" (page 38). It uses mapping a desktop as an introduction to map-making.

Concepts
Objects are to have the same relationship to one another in the drawing as they do on the desk.

Skills
• Observing
• Representing the observation
• Comparing the order of things observed to their representation

Standards
Benchmarks for Science Literacy: #1B, #2C

Standards for the English Language Arts: #12

Principles and Standards for School Mathematics: Com2, G2

National Science Education Standards: A

Curriculum Standards for Social Studies: #3

Time Needed
45 minutes to 1 hour

Materials
• Student notebooks
• Pencils
• Paper
• Other objects to place on desks (pencil sharpeners, textbooks, rulers, glue sticks, other familiar classroom supplies)

Procedure
1. Have each student place a notebook, a pencil, and one other item on their desktop in any arrangement. For example:

   • Closed notebook at the left edge of the desk; pencil close to the notebook on the right; pencil sharpener directly below the pencil

   • Open notebook with a pencil in spine with a ruler placed horizontally below the notebook

   • Textbook sitting on top of the open notebook in the center of the desk; pencil on top of the textbook

2. Have students prepare to map the items on their desks by asking them to describe how they have placed objects on their desks. Help them clarify their descriptions by asking questions of distance and direction:

   • Is the pencil closer to the notebook or to the side of the desk?

   • Is the pencil to the right or left of the notebook?

   • Where is the ruler in relation to the notebook?

3. Have the children draw (make a map of) their desktop and the objects on it.

4. Display the children's maps and have them talk about what they saw and how they translated their observations into a map.

5. Ask children to describe how the maps would be different if drawn from a side view, with eyes at the level of the desk top.

Activity № 11

Map Your Room

Grade Level
2 and up; all experiential levels

Purpose
To get started with mapping by mapping a familiar space, then analyzing ways to represent objects and spaces

Overview
This is a popular activity that meets learners on their own territory. Used as a vehicle for getting students started with mapping, this activity is one that they can do on their own and bring into class to share with their classmates. It can also be used as an assessment or baseline measure of students' skills with making maps.

Concepts
- Any area can be mapped.
- The map of an area shows the things in the area that are important to the map-maker.
- The map of an area shows where things are located in relation to one another.

Skills
- Observing and recording data
- Analyzing (comparing and contrasting) data

Standards
Benchmarks for Science Literacy: #1B, #2C

Standards for the English Language Arts: #12

Principles and Standards for School Mathematics: Com2, C3, G1, G2

National Science Education Standards: A

Curriculum Standards for Social Studies: #3

Time Needed
Homework time, plus 1 class period

Materials
- Students' maps of their own rooms
- Chart paper
- Marker

Procedure
1. Give students this homework assignment:
   - Draw a map of your room at home. Show the things in your room and how they are arranged.

   If necessary, allow extra time for those who haven't finished the assignment so that everyone has a map to work with.

2. When everyone has a map, divide students in pairs or small groups.

3. Have students discuss the similarities and differences in their maps, such as:
   - things included in the map
   - use of color
   - many details or few details
   - labels or no labels
   - side views, top views, and combinations of these

4. Post students' maps around the room.

5. Bring the whole class together to discuss what students observed in their small groups. Record on chart paper the similarities and differences that the students describe.

6. For homework, have students create revised maps of their rooms, incorporating ideas they have gained from this activity.

Strategies/Tips

- This is an excellent time to introduce the ideas of point of view and, in particular, the bird's-eye view, as well as the use of symbols and legends on maps.

- The instructions for this activity can be adapted to your students' skills and developmental levels. One teacher asked students not to include anything on the walls; another gave them the option of showing side or top views. If you use this as a tool for assessing what students already know and understand about mapping, keep directions to a minimum.

Activity № 12

Find North

Grade Level
3-5

Purpose
To explore tools and techniques for locating, identifying, and using cardinal directions

Overview
Students learn about cardinal directions and how to use a compass to determine directions.

Concepts
- The cardinal directions are based on the Earth's magnetic field.
- A compass is a tool for determining which direction is north.
- A compass rose indicates the cardinal directions on a map.
- Knowing the cardinal directions is useful in certain situations.

Skills
- Using a compass
- Reading a compass rose on a map

Standards
Benchmarks for Science Literacy: #1B, #2A

Standards for the English Language Arts: #7

Principles and Standards for School Mathematics: G1, G2

National Science Education Standards: A, E

Curriculum Standards for Social Studies: #3

Time Needed
1 class period

Materials
- Pencils
- Erasers
- Small teacher-made map of classroom showing fixed features
- Directional compasses (one for each child)
- Book: *Follow the Drinking Gourd*
- Chart paper
- Marker
- Signs for the classroom walls: "North," "South," "East," "West"

Procedure
1. Read aloud or have students read *Follow the Drinking Gourd*.

2. Discuss the book, with an emphasis on the importance of directions in the story. Start by asking questions like these:
   - Why was it important for the people in the book to know which way was north? (They had to travel north in order to escape slavery.)
   - How did they know which way was north? (They used the stars in the Big Dipper.)

3. Ask students to point to north. (Students are likely to point in different directions, including up.) Ask individuals to explain why they pointed in a certain direction. Record their answers on chart paper. Then ask, How can we figure out which way is really north? Again, record their answers on chart paper.

4. Explain to students that they are going to learn how to use a compass to determine directions: north, south, east, and west.

5. Give each child a map of the classroom and a compass.

6. Ask students to describe what happens to the compass as they stand in one place, hold the compass in front of them, and turn their bodies in different directions while keeping the hand holding the compass still. (Help students notice that the red end of the needle always points in the same direction.)

7. Explain to students that a compass needle is really a magnet, balanced so it can turn and line itself up with the Earth's magnetic field. When it does this, the red end of the needle points north.

8. Have students look at their compasses and then point in the direction of north—the direction the red end of the needle is pointing. Then have them turn so that they are facing north—moving their feet as they turn but keeping the hand holding the compass still. Ask volunteers to describe the relationship between the red end of the compass needle and the letter N on the compass face. (They are lined up or nearly lined up.) Explain that lining up the needle and the letter N is called orienting the compass.

9. As students are facing north with the red end of the compass needle aligned with the N, ask them to look at their compasses and...

- Point east.
- Point west.
- Point south.

Summarize what students are observing by explaining that when a compass is oriented so that the needle is aligned with N, it is possible to use it to find the other directions, too.

10. Once again ask students to point to the north side of the room. Then have them look at the classroom map and point to the north side of the room on the map.

11. Ask students to orient the map to the compass directions by following these steps:

- Place the map on a table or the floor so that the north side of the room on the map is facing the north side of the room.
- Place the compass on the map and turn it so that the red end of the needle is lined up with the N on the compass face.

12. Finally, ask students to draw a compass rose—a circle showing north, south, east, and west—on the classroom map. Then place signs on the walls of the classroom to correspond to the directions: "North," "South," "East," "West."

Strategies/Tips

- Make sure that the compasses are working properly. Some needles may have switched polarity so that the red end of the needle does not point north.

- When students are working with the compasses, keep them away from metal tables, desks, chairs, cabinets, and other large metal objects that could disrupt the accuracy of the compasses.

Activity № 13

The Smartest Gerbils

Grade Level
2-5

Purpose
To determine students' understanding of maps and their ability to make maps.

Overview
An imaginary scenario is used to motivate students to create maps of the classroom: Helping the pet gerbils make the most of the classroom facilities and find their way back to the cage by morning. This activity provides a useful tool for assessing students' understanding of maps and their map-making skills.

Concepts
This is a diagnostic activity to see the level of children's mapping skills and the nature of their mapping concepts.

Skills
• Observing
• Comparing
• Use of proportion
• Representing physical space on a map

Standards
Benchmarks for Science Literacy: #1B, #2C

Standards for the English Language Arts: #7

Principles and Standards for School Mathematics: G1, G2

National Science Education Standards: A

Time Needed
1 class period

Materials
• Pencils
• Crayons
• Paper
• Graph paper
• Rulers

Note: At the lower grades this has been used as a fun way to assess children's ideas about maps and their map-making abilities. In grades 4-6 this activity can be used to facilitate skill development in directionality, coordinates, ratios and proportions, symbols, and distinguishing among types of maps. Maps can be saved for comparative post-assessment after completion of mapping curriculum.

Procedure
1. Read this to the class and/or write it on the board:

   "Imagine that our gerbils (or other class pets) are allowed to roam the room freely at night. They can visit the different parts of the room and use the things they find there, just as we do. However, there is a problem: They get lost because they have no maps to guide them around the room and then back to their home. You're going to make a map for them. We'll place all the maps around the room to help our pets find their way."

2. Give no directions or suggestion on how to do this mapping except to tell students who feel overwhelmed that they can begin with a section of the room. Make clear that crayons and other materials that they need will be made available. Stress that you are not looking for perfection nor any specific type of map. Students should include those things they think are important.

3. Provide graph paper grids as well as blank paper. This will provide a choice for those who may know how to use grids for more refined mapping.

4. When they are finished, have the students discuss their work and describe what they did to the rest of the class.

5. Whatever students produce is fine and is an indicator of their map-making skills. The teacher can assess skill areas to target based on what students talk about and produce.

6. At this time, the teacher can review and discuss a few commonly found maps (e.g.: city maps, USA map, a globe, zoo maps, fire exit maps, etc.)

Strategies/Tips

• As an introductory mapping activity, this may stimulate students questions such as:

• How can I figure out how to put things in their right order?

• How do I figure our where north is?

Activity № 14

Desk Maps

Grade Level
3-6

Purpose
To create maps that communicate clearly

Overview
Making their desk maps gets students to note the differences in the shapes of objects carefully and to record them. Students exchange their detailed maps and try to locate each random arrangement based on the maps.

Concepts
Representations of objects on a map correspond to objects that exist in physical space. Maps show relative positions of objects and locations in the space they represent.

Skills
• Understanding and representing perspective on a map
• Understanding and representing correspondence on a map
• Understanding dimensions
• Representing dimensions and distances proportionally on a map

Standards
Benchmarks for Science Literacy: #1B, #2C

Standards for the English Language Arts: #7, #12

Principles and Standards for School Mathematics: Com1, Com2, G1, G2

National Science Education Standards: A

Time Needed
1-2 class periods

Materials
• Graph paper
• Pencils
• For each cluster of 4 student desks, a group of objects such as:
  • pencil
  • coat hanger
  • soda can
  • wooden block
  • paper clip
  • book
  • glue stick
  • cup

Procedure
1. Divide students into groups of four and arrange each groups' desks together in a cluster.
2. Distribute object collections and graph paper to each group.
3. Have students arrange the objects on their grouped desks, then map the desktop. Tell students they should NOT write their names on their maps.
4. Collect the desk maps as they are completed and redistribute them to students from other groups.
5. Students use the maps to identify the group where the map was made.
6. Bring the class together to discuss students' work and observations.
   • What characteristics of the map made it easy to locate the desk?
   • What made it difficult?
   • Did the map-maker use the grid on the graph paper to show the location of each desk and the objects on it?

- How well did the map identify each desk in a group?

- How well did the map represent which objects were on which desk?

- What was the effect of the pattern in which the group arranged the objects?

- What was the effect of the perspective from which the map was drawn?

- What was the effect of the way the map-maker oriented features on the map?

- What was the effect of the way the map-maker represented the proportionality of the objects in relation to their actual proportions and locations?

Extensions

- Take pictures of the classroom or another familiar location. Give the pictures to students and ask them to try to identify the locations from which the photographs were taken.

- Divide the class into pairs of students. Place a barrier between the two students. One student describes his/her area while the other student draws a map using only the information provided by his/her partner.

Activity №15

Brainstorming: What Can We Map?

Grade Level
3 and up (requires knowledge of traditional maps)

Purpose
To get students to think of other kinds of maps beyond road, state, and country maps

Overview
This activity encourages students who already know about traditional maps to think about all the things they might represent spatially. The resulting lists include places, routes, and all sorts of data.

Concepts
Maps can represent all kinds of spaces, and things or quantities related to those spaces.

Skills
• Brainstorming

• Representing things on a map

Standards
Benchmarks for Science Literacy: #1B, #2C

Standards for the English Language Arts: #12

Principles and Standards for School Mathematics: Com1, Com2

National Science Education Standards: A

Time Needed
1 class period

Materials
• Chart paper

• Markers

• Sample maps—e.g., road maps, route maps (such as those showing the way to the exit or bus routes); topographical maps; weather maps; museum or zoo maps, etc.

Procedure
1. Gather students around the display of sample maps. Ask students to describe each of the maps and what they show. Stay with each map long enough to deal with the details. For example, most road maps include information about the type of road, the size of city, the location of airports, and much more. Begin the brainstorming with questions like these:

• What kind of things could you map?

• What places could you map?

• What thing going on in those places could you show on a map?

• What could you map about animals: in our class? in the zoo? in the wild?

• What invisible things might we map (e.g., temperature)?

2. Record all the examples given on chart paper. (See sample brainstorming list on page 65.)

3. When you are satisfied with the scope of the list, have students review it and identify items they think may not belong on the list. Discuss how the questioned items might be mapped, what the difficulties might be, or why it does not lend itself to mapping.

Sample Brainstorming Results from Activity #15

Animal habitat

Animal migration

Animal life cycles

Bedroom

Best sections in supermarkets

Birth places of students in the class

Bodies of water

Books read

Camping trip

Choreography/dances

Classrooms

Closets

Clouds

Compare travel paths

Criminal activities

Currency

Desks and chairs

Dinosaurs

Doors in building

Eating establishments

Ecosystems

Electrical circuits

Elevation

Emotions

Empty lot(s)

Endangered or threatened species

Energy power plants

Family, ethnicity, culture

Favorite areas in museums

Fire escapes

Fire drill route

Food origins

Food in supermarket

Fossils

Fun places

Games

Gardens

Going to/from lunchroom, bathroom, office

Going to/from school

Grades

Imaginary trip

Immigration

Jobs

Kitchen

Landmarks

Languages

Library

Lunch tray

Lunchroom food route

Mechanisms

Metamorphosis

Moon and sun patterns

Museum and their routes

Neighborhood

Parking lot and its cars

People's routes in supermarkets

Pet environment and its travel patterns

Plants and their root systems

Playground(s)

Points of interest

Recycling

Refrigerator

Renovation of a building

Route on trips

Route to the supermarket

Scary places

School

School routes

Activity № 16

The Route to School

Grade Level
4-6

Purpose
To develop skills in making and evaluating route maps: symbols, landmarks, and orientating devices in maps of large-scale areas

Overview
Some maps are designed for the purpose of explaining how to get somewhere. These maps are like instruction manuals that tell the user how to get a job done. Adults make a map of this sort when they provide a route map showing how to get to one's house or a social function. This activity gives children the chance to make that kind of map— one that shows how they get from home to school.

Concepts
Symbols, landmarks, and compass roses are devices used on maps to give users necessary information.

Skills
Making and using maps

Standards
Benchmarks for Science Literacy: #1A, #1B, #12D

Standards for the English Language Arts: #12

Principles and Standards for School Mathematics: PS2, PS3, Com1, Com2, G1, G2, M1, M2

National Science Education Standards A

Curriculum Standards for Social Studies #3

Time Needed
15 minutes to introduce homework plus 1 class period

Materials
• Children's maps produced as homework

• Chart paper

• Marker

Procedure
1. Tell students that for homework they are going to make a map that shows how to get from their home to school. Give students a chance to ask questions about what's involved in making this kind of map—e.g.:

   • "Do I have to show all the buildings?"

   • "How do I show where I'm on the bus?"

   Encourage children to figure out how to solve these problems in ways that others can understand when they see their maps.

2. Show students examples of other maps. Point out how symbols are used to show hospitals, airports, parks, and the like. To help students begin to think about the elements they'll include on their maps, ask questions such as

   • What kinds of things do you pass on your way to school that you might want to have symbols for on your map?

   • How can you show directions on your map?

   • How can you show where your route starts and where it ends?

3. When students have finished the homework assignment, post the maps on walls around the room.

4. Have a discussion about how you can tell if a map does what its maker intended— in this case, show how one person gets from home to school. Record students' criteria on chart paper—e.g.:

   • "It makes sense."

   • "I can tell where her home is."

   • "I know which way she turns, which streets she walks on."

   • "I can tell which stores she passes."

   • "The labels are clear."

5. Give students the chance to revise or redesign their maps using the criteria you've recorded.

Activity № 17

Route to a Destination Within the Classroom

Grade Level
4-6; novice to experienced in making maps

Purpose
To further develop skills in making and evaluating route maps

Overview
Students create route maps using their classroom environment, which provides opportunities for them to begin to establish criteria for evaluating the effectiveness of a route map.

Concepts
- Perspective, orientation, and scale are tools for making effective maps.
- Maps are evaluated based on how well they communicate what the map-maker intended to map-users.

Skills
Using scale/proportion accurately in a map

Standards
Benchmarks for Science Literacy: #1B, #12D

Standards for the English Language Arts: #6, #7

Principles and Standards for School Mathematics: PS2, PS3, Com1, Com2, G1, G2, M1, M2

National Science Education Standards: A

Curriculum Standards for Social Studies: #3

Time Needed
2 class periods

Materials
- Paper
- Pencils
- Markers or crayons
- Rulers

Procedure
1. Review students' "Route To School" maps and discuss what made some maps more successful than others

2. Discuss the role of scale, perspective, and orientation in making maps that work.

   - To help students understand scale, ask them to describe different items in the classroom in terms of their relative sizes—e.g., the teacher's desk and a student's desk; an eraser and a book.

   - To review perspective, have students take turns describing how the same thing looks from different points of view. Then remind them that on a map, everything on the map must be shown from the same point of view.

   - For orientation, review the four cardinal directions and how they can be used to help someone orient directions on a map to the physical world.

3. Give students this assignment:

    Make a map that shows the route to follow in the classroom in order to do a particular task—for example, going from your desk to the water fountain. Use START, END, and cardinal directions on your map. Your map should be able to be read by others in the class.

4. As soon as students finish their maps, have them exchange maps with a class-mate so that each can try out the other's map.

5. After all maps have been tried, gather the class for a discussion, starting with questions like these:

    • What qualities made maps easy to follow?

    • What qualities made maps more difficult to follow?

    • How did the maps use words?

    • How did the maps use symbols?

Strategies/Tips

It may be necessary for students to do a few "dry runs" before actually making their maps. It takes practice to make readable maps. Give students opportunities to revise and redraw their maps, and to make different kinds of maps.

Activity № 18

Making a Master Map: Establishing Scale

Grade Level
4-6

Purpose
To develop understanding of scale (what scale is, which scale is appropriate)

Overview
Students determine a workable scale for creating a large classroom map. This activity results in a "master map"—a teacher-made representation, drawn to scale on graph paper, of the perimeter of the room.

Concepts
• To map to scale is to have all measures in the map be in the same ratio to the comparable measures in the area mapped.

• An appropriate scale is one that results in a map that fills most of the space available for the map.

Skills
Ability to measure and use arithmetic operations, including working with fractions

Standards
Benchmarks for Science Literacy: #1B, #11D

Standards for the English Language Arts: #7

Principles and Standards for School Mathematics: PS2, PS3, Com1, Com2, G1, G2, M1, M2, NO2, NO3

National Science Education Standards: A

Curriculum Standards for Social Studies: #3

Time Needed
60 minutes

Materials
• Student maps from previous classroom mapping activities

• Graph paper and large sheet (24" x 30") of graph paper with 1" squares

• Rulers, yardsticks

• Pencils

Procedure
1. Tell students that you are going to work together to make the most accurate map possible of your classroom. Have a discussion about how to make an accurate map, starting with questions like these:

   • What does it mean to say that a map is accurate?

   • How could a map accurately show the sizes of objects in the room in relation to each other?

   • How could a map accurately show how far apart things are in the room?

2. Review the maps students have previously made: maps showing their routes to school and routes within the classroom:

   • Which maps are easy to understand? Why?

   • How do the easy-to-read signs show the sizes of things in relation to one another?

3. Explain that when things in a map accurately show how big things are in relation to one another, the things are said to be in proportion.

4. Then explain that the way to show things on a map in proportion is to draw them to scale. Explain the concept of scale by giving an example using a 1'=1" scale on graph paper with 1" squares. Suppose you wanted to show a person who is 6 feet tall and a child who is 4 feet tall. If the scale is 1' = 1", then a 6-foot-tall person would be 6 inches tall in the drawing and a 4-foot-tall person would be 4 inches tall. Illustrate this idea on the graph paper. Give another example in which students measure the length of two objects in the classroom—e.g., a table and a bookcase—and then translate those measurements to inches using the 1'=1" scale.

5. When students understand the use of scale in mapping, have students measure the dimensions of a small area of the classroom. Convert the measurements to inches using the 1'=1" scale, and draw the area on graph paper.

6. Continue to explore scale by using different scales to map the same area—e.g., 1'=2" and 2'=1"—and compare them in terms of the space available to make the map. Let students suggest scales and see how they work on the graph paper. The objective is to have students see that the scale determines the size of the paper required to make a map of a space. For example, a scale of 1'=2" requires more space than a scale of 2'=1". For the classroom map, you want to make as large a map as possible on the paper that is available.

7. Following this discussion and demonstration, make a 2'=1" scale map of your classroom on large graph paper showing basic features. In the next class period, show students the map. Let them identify the features and have them measure the features and see the correspondence between the measurements on the map and the actual sizes of things represented on the map.

Activity № 19

Placing Desks on a Master Map

Grade Level
4-6

Purpose
To practice drawing features on a map to scale

Overview
Students add features to the scaled map of the classroom.

Concepts
The map size of a desk has the same ratio to the size of the desk as the map size of the room has to the size of the room. The map size of equal sized desks should be equal.

Skills
- Using a grid to place points on a map
- Measurement
- Understanding ratio, proportion, and scale

Standards
Benchmarks for Science Literacy: 1B, 11D

Standards for the English Language Arts: #7

Principles and Standards for School Mathematics: PS2, PS3, Com1, Com2, G1, G2, M1, M2, NO2, NO3

National Science Education Standards: A

Curriculum Standards for Social Studies: #3

Time Needed
2 or more class periods

Materials
- Graph paper
- Pencils
- Rulers
- Master map to scale (Teacher-made map of the classroom without furniture—see preceding activity)

Procedure
1. Review the work on establishing scale from the preceding activity. Discuss the scale of the master classroom map (2:1). Ask students how they would use that scale to add individual student desks to the classroom map.

2. Assign groups of students whose desks are near each other to work together in teams. Distribute sheets of graph paper to each team. Give this assignment to the teams:

   - Draw your group's desks to a 2:1 scale on your graph paper.

   - Cut out the map of your group of desks.

   - Place this map of your desks in the appropriate area of the master map of the classroom.

3. As groups complete their work have them draw to scale other items of furniture in the room and add them to the Master Map. This may include bookshelves, closets, rugs, computer area, and so forth.

4. When all groups have added their desks to the Master Map, display the map and evaluate it, starting with questions like these:

   • Does any group of desks seem to be the wrong size? If so, what are the clues that make you think that?

   • Does any group of desks seem out of place? If so, what are the clues that make you think that?

   • What problems did you have doing this activity? How did you solve them?

5. If necessary, give teams time to make corrections to the Master Map.

Strategies/Tips

• Carefully observe children during this activity and look for evidence that students do not understand scale. If a team's desk map is not to scale, ask them to compare it to others as they seek to place it on the Master Map.

• Leave the Master Map available for students to add to or adjust as there are changes in the classroom.

Activity № 20

Locating Ourselves in Space

Grade Level
5-8

Purpose
To use two points along adjacent walls to determine a location in the classroom

Overview
This activity introduces middle school learners to using grids. Students visualize an invisible coordinate system to locate and then represent and map themselves in a particular space.

Concepts
A coordinate system makes it possible to pinpoint a location by defining two points on a grid.

Skills
• Graphing

• Mapping

• Using grids

Standards
Benchmarks for Science Literacy: #2C, #12D

Standards for the English Language Arts: #7, #8

Principles and Standards for School Mathematics: G1, G2, M2

National Science Education Standards: A, E

Curriculum Standards for Social Studies: #3

Time Needed
1 class period

Materials
• Pencils

• Paper

• Rulers

• Chart paper

• Marker

Procedure
1. Divide students into small groups.

2. Have each student draw a rough map of the room. Scale is not important as long as the basic shape of the room is maintained. Tell them to include some landmarks along the walls so it's possible to orient the map to the actual room.

3. Ask a student to describe where he or she is sitting in relation to the walls and landmarks in the room. If the student names only one coordinate (e.g., in front of the chalkboard) point out that this description could apply to a large area of the classroom. Point out that two positions are necessary to define precisely where the student is seated. To help students grasp this concept, make a connection to street addresses. If someone is giving you directions to their house, it's not enough for them to say they live on 2nd St. In order for you to find them, you need to know the exact address on 2nd Street in order to pinpoint their location.

4. Have each student in a Group describe his/her location, using 2 room coordinates.

5. Have students pinpoint their location on their room maps by following these steps:

   • Visualize a straight line between your desk and two landmarks in the room. One landmark should be in front or back of you, the other point to your right or left.

   • On your map, draw a straight line from each of the two landmarks.

   • At the place where these lines meet, draw a symbol that stands for your desk.

6. Collect the maps, then redistribute them so that each student has someone else's map.

7. Have students find and sit in the seat that corresponds to the map they have.

8. Have a discussion about using coordinates, starting with questions like these:

   • What made it easy or hard to find the desk on your map?

   • Why did you need two lines to draw your desk on the map?

   • What rules could we write for using landmarks and lines for showing where something is located on a map?

   Record this discussion on chart paper, then have students test the rules and revise them if necessary.

Activity № 21

Mapping a Classroom

Grade Level
5-8

Purpose
To map a space that will later be used to collect data on diffusion

Overview
Students develop a scale map of the classroom that will be used for additional activities as a data collection tool. This activity makes use of a short-cut: a teacher-made 8-1/2" x 11"scale map of the class-room perimeter. This reduces the time needed for map-making to one period or less, yet assures that students have the basic notion of locating a point on a grid.

Concepts
- Coordinate systems make it possible to locate a point on a map.
- Drawing a map to scale means that the relative sizes of things on the map correspond to their relative sizes in the real world.

Skills
Using grids

Standards
Benchmarks for Science Literacy: #2C, #11D, #12D

Standards for the English Language Arts: #7, #8

Principles and Standards for School Mathematics: PS2, PS3, Com2, G2, M1, M2

National Science Education Standards: A, E

Curriculum Standards for Social Studies: #3

Time Needed
1 class period

Materials
- Teacher-made to-scale map of the classroom perimeter on 8-1/2"x11" graph paper (4-5 squares per inch)
- Pencils
- Rulers

Procedure
1. Distribute the scale maps of the class perimeter and tell students the scale. Describe how you measured the perimeter of the room and then drew it to scale. Tell the students that they will complete the map by drawing in their desks.

2. Ask the class, "How can you determine where to draw your desk on this map, and how do you know how big to draw it?" Guide the students to an understanding of the task by discussing the size of the desk in terms of its length and width and how to translate those dimensions to the map scale. Use the teacher's desk as an example:

   - Locate a point on the front wall from which a line, perpendicular to the wall, will pass through the corner of the teacher's desk. Repeat for a point on the side wall. Measure the distance of each point to the nearest corner of the room.

   - Measure the distance from the corner of the desk to the two points identified above.

- Convert these measurements to the map scale.

- Plot the wall points on the map. Draw perpendiculars on the map from these points to where they cross. This is where the corner of the desk is on their map. Double check by comparing the distance to the wall from the crossing point to the measured distance to the wall.

- Draw the remainder of the desk, to scale.

- Then have them draw the teacher's desk to scale on their maps.

3. Have students follow the above procedure to locate the coordinates of the front left hand corner of their desks in terms of distances from points on adjoining walls.

4. As each student reports the location of his/her desk in turn, all students record the location of the desk on their maps.

5. Students complete the map by drawing in all the desks.

Activity №22

Mapping Diffusion in a Petri Dish

Grade Level
5-8

Purpose
To apply mapping techniques to describe the process of diffusion through a liquid

Overview
Students observe, record, and map the spread of food coloring as it approaches the outer portion of a Petri dish. This is an example of diffusion and is a good introduction to the concept.

Concepts
Mapping techniques can be used to document the diffusion of color through a liquid over time.

Skills
• Understanding of diffusion
• Measurement
• Mapping
• Use of grids

Standards
Benchmarks for Science Literacy: #1D, #11A, #12A, #12D

Standards for the English Language Arts: #7

Principles and Standards for School Mathematics: PS2, G2, M2

National Science Education Standards: A, E

Time Needed
2 class periods

Materials
For each group of students:
• 1 Petri dish cover or bottom
• Blank white paper for each student in the group
• Small container for water
• Coloring pencils (one color)
• Ruler
• Clock or watch
• Food coloring
• Chart paper

Procedure
Divide students into small groups and provide each group with a set of materials.

A. Preparation by Students
Each student in the group will:

1. Place your group's Petri dish in the middle of your sheet of paper and trace the circular outline of the dish.

2. Measure the diameter of the circular outline of the dish you have drawn.

3. Identify the center of the circle and make a line through it to the edges of the circle.

4. Mark the line at half-centimeter intervals beginning at the center and marking outward.

5. Label the center mark "0". On either side of the center "0" label each centimeter mark consecutively. (Your teacher will demonstrate this on the chalkboard.)

6. When everyone has made a drawing, place the Petri dish on top of one of the drawings. The others will be used by group members to map diffusion.

B. Preparation by Teacher

1. Prepare two liters of a mixture of water and detergent (about 1 teaspoon of detergent per liter of water). Try not to produce suds in the process; the detergent is simply there to break down the surface tension of the water, which can confuse students by causing wacky things to happen to the food coloring. (Try it yourself to see what happens without the detergent!) Water should be at room temperature when the activity begins in order to minimize convection currents in the Petri dish.

2. Give each group about 50cc of the solution.

3. Depending on your resources and your students, either give each group a supply of food coloring and a medicine dropper, or simply place the drops of food coloring yourself in the water in the Petri dishes.

C. Carrying Out the Experiment

1. Warn students NOT to move the table AT ALL. (Note: Jiggling the desk will move the food coloring more than the forces of diffusion will. Thus the results will be confused.)

2. Place approximately 40ml. of the prepared water in the Petri dish. (The amount of prepared water depends on the size of the Petri dish. Use just enough to cover the bottom completely and then some.) Allow the water to settle and remind students NOT to move the table AT ALL.

3. Place a drop of food coloring in the center of the Petri dish.

4. Students should immediately draw a line that represents the actual size of the food coloring.

5. On one piece of paper, have students draw a picture of what they think the Petri dish will look like after 5 minutes. Label this drawing "Prediction."

6. After 5 minutes, ask students to draw a line representing the expansion of the food coloring in the Petri dish.

7. Repeat at 5-minute intervals for approximately 15 minutes, or as long as students can sustain interest and concentration. Label lines "5," "10," "15," as appropriate.

8. Use a colored pencil to show how the food coloring gets progressively lighter as it approaches the outer portion of the Petri dish. (Simply bearing down harder or lighter on the pencil will produce an infinite variety of shades of color).

9. At the end of the period, allow 15-20 minutes to have students transfer their drawings to chart paper. Display the different maps around the room and have students inspect each others' work.

D. Discussion

1. Give students the chance to inspect all of the maps. Then have a discussion about the results, starting with questions like these:

   • Why don't all of the maps look exactly the same? Which maps illustrate that the experiment was carried out correctly? (Stress that each map is correct to the extent that it depicts what actually happened.)

- Can you figure out which groups stayed calm and did not bump their table? How do you know?

- What would it look like if the experiment were done with absolutely calm water and no breeze?

2. Based on their understanding of diffusion of food coloring in a liquid, have students represent a map of a perfectly done experiment.

Strategies/Tips

- Use red, blue, or green food coloring. Yellow is too light.

- Have some topics for discussion or other activities available to occupy students while they are waiting for diffusion to occur. It is a slow process, but that's also part of the point of this activity —to demonstrate that the speed (or slowness) of diffusion is a limitation on the size of cells.

Activity № 23

Mapping Diffusion of Gas in the Classroom

Grade Level
5-8

Purpose
To use mapping techniques to visually represent an invisible process

Overview
Students make visual representations of an invisible process as they record, then map, the time it takes for the odor of strong perfume to radiate out from the bottle and spread throughout the room.

Concepts
Mapping techniques can be used to document a physical process over time.

Skills
• Knowledge of contour mapping
• Understanding of what molecules are and how they behave
• Understanding of diffusion
• Understanding of gases, convection, and concentration

Standards
Benchmarks for Science Literacy: #1D, #11A, #12A, #12D

Standards for the English Language Arts: #7

Principles and Standards for School Mathematics: PS2, G2, M2

National Science Education Standards: A, E

Time Needed
3-4 45-minute class periods

Materials
• Individual student maps of classroom from Activity #21.
• Air freshener or potent perfume
• Colored pencils
• Clock or watch

Procedure
1. Students should be evenly distributed throughout the classroom. Each student should have a map of the classroom from Activity #21.

2. Use the master map developed in the previous activity or draw a large rough map of the room on the chalkboard or chart paper including the location of the desks. The map needs to be large enough so that you can make three notations at each desk location.

3. Have a discussion with the class about gas, making the point that gases are invisible but their presence can be detected by their odor. Explain that the purpose of this activity is to track and map the diffusion over time of an invisible gas through the classroom.

4. Describe this procedure for the experiment:

   • The teacher will open a container of air freshener or perfume at the front of the room.

   • The teacher will immediately begin counting at five-second intervals (5, 10, 15, 20, etc.).

   • As soon as you smell the air freshener, write down the time that you hear the teacher call out.

   • When the air freshener has had time to diffuse through-out the entire room, you will be asked to share your data.

   • The times for your desk location will be recorded on the large map.

- Once the air freshener or perfume is closed and while the room is being aired out, you will switch seat places repeat the procedure.

- After the second data collection, the room will be cleared of odor, seats switched, and the procedure repeated a third time.

- You will then take an average diffusion time for each desk location in the room.

- You will plot this data on your individual maps, using a color code similar to weather maps. This will give a picture of how the gas travels.

- You might want students to predict what the maps will look like, particularly if they have already done the Petri dish activity.

5. Before beginning the activity, make sure everyone recognizes the odor to be identified. Make sure the room is free of the odor before beginning.

6. Place the bottle on a table or desk in the front of the room, open it, and immediately begin counting off five-second intervals.

7. When all students have detected the odor, collect the data from each student and record it for that desk location.

8. Clear the odor from the room and repeat two more times.

9. Examine the data from the three trials and discuss it, starting with questions like these:

   - Why did I have you change places for each trial? (Different students have sensitivity to odors.)

   - Why do you think there are the differences in the data?

   - How shall we decide the time to map for each location?

10. Have students record the average time (or median, depending on the group's decision) on their own maps, for each desk location.

11. Have students draw contour lines at 10 second intervals. (Teachers may need to direct this part of the activity if contour mapping has not yet been learned.)

12. Have students color-code their maps using a system similar to weather maps. Here is one scheme:

    Brown - Dark Red - Light Red - Dark Orange - Light Orange - Yellow - Dark Green - Light Green - Dark Blue - Light Blue - Dark Purple - Light Purple - Gray - White.

13. Post students' maps around the room. Have students compare and discuss them:

    - Should they all look the same?

    - Which ways of mapping the times are most effective? (This evaluative question is to help students think about effective ways of presenting map data)

    - How does this activity compare with the Petri dish activity?

    - Should all the maps look similar?

    - What might account for the differences from the Petri dish map? (The reasons might include beginning the diffusion from the end of a rectangular space rather than the middle of a round one, differences in diffusion patterns between gases and liquids, differences in sensitivity to smell, errors in detecting the smell, convection currents in the room, drafts, etc.).

    - Talk about the similarities and differences in the students' work.

Strategies/Tips

Pick a comfortable day when the heat is off and the windows can be closed. This will reduce drafts and convection currents within the room. You might also try arranging desks in a circular pattern so as to replicate the pattern seen in the Petri dish activity.

Standards for Activities

Benchmarks for Science Literacy

1A

Results of similar scientific investigations seldom turn out exactly the same. Sometimes this is because of unexpected differences in the things being investigated.

1B

1. People can often learn about things around them by just observing those things carefully.

2. Describing things as accurately as possible is important in science because it enables people to compare their observations with those of others.

3. Scientific investigations may take many different forms, including observing what things are like or what is happening somewhere ... and doing experiments.

2A

1. Mathematics is the study of many kinds of patterns, including numbers and shapes and operations on them.

2. Patterns are studied because they help to explain how the world works or how to solve practical problems.

2C

1. Mathematicians often represent things with abstract ideas, such as numbers and straight lines.

2. In using math, choices have to be made about what operations will give the best results. Results should always be judged by whether they make sense and are useful.

11A

1. In something that consists of many parts, the parts usually influence one another.

2. A system can include processes as well as things.

11D

1. Almost everything has limits on how big or small it can be made.

12A

1. Raise questions about the world around and be willing to seek answers to some of them by making careful observations and trying things out.

2. Keep records of investigations and observations and not change the records later.

3. Offer reasons for findings and consider reasons suggested by others.

12D

1. Write instructions that others can follow in carrying out a procedure.

2. Make sketches to aid in explaining procedures or ideas.

3. Use numerical data in describing and comparing objects and events.

Standards for the English Language Arts

4. Students adjust their use of spoken, written and visual language . . . to communicate effectively with a variety of audiences and for different purposes.

6. Students apply knowledge of language structure, language conventions, media techniques, figurative language, and genre to create, critique, and discuss print and nonprint texts.

7. Students conduct research . . . by generating ideas and questions, and by posing problems. They gather, evaluate, and synthesize data from a variety of sources (e.g., print and non print texts, artifacts, people) to communicate their discoveries in ways that suit their purpose and audience.

8. Students use a variety of technological and informational resources to gather and synthesize information and to create and communicate knowledge.

12. Students use spoken, written, and visual language to accomplish their own purposes.

Principles and Standards for School Mathematics

Problem Solving

    PS1:   Solve problems that arise in mathematics and in other contexts.

    PS3:   Apply and adapt a variety of appropriate strategies to solve problems.

Communication

    Com1: Organize and consolidate their mathematical thinking through communication.

    Com2: Communicate their mathematical thinking coherently and clearly to peers, teachers, and others.

Connections

    C3:   Recognize and apply mathematics in contexts outside of mathematics.

Representation

R1:   Create and use representations to organize, record, and communicate mathematical ideas.

Measurement

M1:   Understand measurable attributes of objects and the units, systems, and processes of measurement.

M2:   Apply appropriate techniques, tools, and formulas to determine measurements.

Data Analysis and Probability

DA&P1: Formulate questions that can be addressed with data and collect, organize, and display relevant data to answer them.

Geometry

G1:   Analyze characteristics and properties of two- and three-dimensional geometric shapes and develop mathematical arguments about geometric relationships.

G2:   Specify locations and describe spatial relationships using coordinate geometry and other representational systems.

Numerical Operations

NO2:   Understand meanings of operations and how they relate to one another.

NO3:   Compute fluently and make reasonable estimates.

National Science Education Standards

A: Students should develop abilities necessary to do scientific inquiry.

E: Students should develop abilities of technological design and understand about science and technology.

Curriculum Standards for Social Studies

3. People, Places and Environments

Social studies programs should include experiences that provide for the study of people, places, and environments.

Mapping in the Elementary Grades

Map Brainstorming and a Map Scavenger Hunt

There are two excellent starting activities for any new technology curriculum topic: a scavenger hunt and brainstorming. In scavenger hunts, students enjoy looking for examples of things, and will often compete to find more than anyone else. They look in classrooms, corridors, and elsewhere in the school. They look for examples on field trips, on the way home, and at home. A brainstorming session is the mental version of a scavenger hunt. It is a search for ideas from one's own experience and imagination.

Minerva Rivera is a first-year teacher of the only fourth grade class of a small alternative school in East Harlem, New York City. She began her mapping lesson by asking students to define a map. Here are some of their answers:

DAN:
A paper with color on it (like a weather map).

NICOLE R.:
Something that tells you where to go... like a movie map. It tells you what movie you want to see.

DARRYL:
Something that tells you where the states are.

GABRIEL:
A piece of paper with a bunch of information on it.

JULIAN:
A map is something that's like a menu that shows you different stuff.

JILLIEN:
A piece of paper that tells you where to go (like a different city).

MAGALIE:
It shows you where to go so you won't get lost (like an exit).

RICHARD:
Something to show you where somebody lives.

TENAYA:
I think a map is like a big piece of paper that shows where to go so you won't get hurt.

After this preliminary brainstorming session, Minerva asked her students to bring in examples from newspapers of what they considered "maps."

All of the items were tabulated and listed on the blackboard. This is what the list looked like:

weather maps (5)	sports information	TV listings (3)
job listings	apartment listings	index to the newspaper
movie listings	stock quotes	a train map
an atlas	a road map	a zoo map
a traffic map	a US map	

Some children challenged whether all of these items could really be considered maps. In her reflections Minerva wrote:

The discussion that this assignment brought about was very enlightening. The children were beginning to question what a map should provide you with.

The following day, the list of maps from the assignment was still up on the blackboard. Minerva distributed newspapers and asked her students to look for kinds of maps that were not already listed.

The kids made a mess, were loud and very productive. It was great fun for them! I gave them all the time they needed. I walked around from group to group and asked them why they had made particular choices. Once they were done, I asked each group to present their findings.

The following items were listed on the blackboard:

cartoons	a graph of stock prices
an ad showing prices and pictures of computer models	theater listings
menus	a calendar of sports events
results of a poll about TV shows	supermarket specials
	a tide chart

Minerva described the sharing session:

There was a bit of an uproar when one particular group presented their poster. They said cartoons can be considered maps and there were some kids who challenged that. One child defended the group by stating that it was "a map of words and pictures." This activity worked well in providing the students with food for thought. It was difficult for me to say whether the cartoon people were right or wrong, because I myself had no clear definition as to whether their work could be considered a map.

Probing further, Minerva challenged her children to explain what maps are and what they are used for. The class had the following dialogue:

SHONA:
My group doesn't think a cartoon is a map. It doesn't show you where to go. What does it have to do with directions?

JULIAN:

Maps don't have to show you where to go. It's exchanging dialogue.

TENAYA:

It does have something to do with direction. First they have to draw it out. It's saying stuff. It is a map. Look at it!

NYOSHA:

It can be a dialog, but it's not a map. A menu is a map, but it's also a dialog map.

NICHOLE:

A map is not fiction. Cartoons are fiction.

TENAYA:

Not all maps are not fiction.

DARRYL:

If a map is fiction, then whatever is on it is not true.

DORIS:

Cartoons are not a map because they don't tell you anything.

JULIAN:

It is a word map. It is a dialog map.

NYOSHA:

How can you decide yourself the sure definition of a map?

Following this discussion, Minerva asked the class a related question:

"What should every map have?"

This would give them a way of classifying things according to whether or not they contained the elements of a map. The following items were listed:

places, numbers,
dots (designate places)
date, title
data, lines, words,
symbols and directions

The class then re-assembled into the original groups. Their task was to determine which of the items from the Map Scavenger Hunt met the criteria they had developed. After the groups met, they reported their conclusions to the entire class; according to whether they were "maps" or "not maps."

Maps	Not Maps
Weather map	TV & movie listings
Train map	Stock quotes
Newspaper index	Cartoons
Road maps	Sports results
Zoo map	Menus
Apartment listings	

This unit hints at some of the richness contained in the deceptively simple question "What is a map?" Children find maps fascinating because they convey a lot of information all at once, and because maps frequently contain interesting twists and surprises. As ways of presenting and learning ideas, maps seem more exciting and immediate than words. Minerva's assignment released some of this excitement. Her students looked around for items that hold some of the same interest as maps and perhaps share some of the characteristics. But are they really maps? They debated this question because they couldn't really agree on the definition of a map. Nyosha pointed out this difficulty in her question, "How can you decide yourself the sure definition of a map?"

Mapping with a Broad Brush

So, what is a map? Adults don't agree on this question either. In everyday language, map usually means a drawing showing how things are arranged in space. The way they are arranged in the drawing is supposed to show how they are really arranged in the world. This type of map should really be called a *geographical map,* because it uses graphic images to indicate geographical relationships. This narrow definition of map was the one used by Shona and Nichole when they claimed a map should "show you where to go" and not be fiction.

On the other hand, there are many precedents for using the word *map* in a broader sense. Teachers use the *concept map* to describe a picture showing how abstract concepts are related. Educational psychologists use the terms *mental map* and *cognitive map* to suggest the way the mind represents information. It is sometimes used as a metaphor for an organized plan, as when one "maps out" one's future. Similarly, the term *road map* suggests any kind of plan or even a guideline for behavior, as in "The union contract is the road map to the rights of labor and management." These broader notions of mapping are no more far-fetched than Tenaya and Julian's idea that a comic strip is a map of an exchange of dialogue. A comic strip may not show direction in the sense of getting you somewhere, but it certainly does have a direction in time, from beginning to end.

In *Mapping,* we will mainly be looking at maps as defined by the narrower, geographical meaning, but there are good reasons to explore the broader meaning as well. Concept maps, menus, comic strips, movie listings, newspaper ads, and so on, do share something in common with geographical maps. All of them use symbols and relative positions on the page to represent or refer to something in the world. In the case of geographical maps, this "something" consists of real relationships in space. Concept maps represent the relationships among ideas; menus, the organization of a meal; and comic strips, the relationships and flow of dialogue among fictitious characters. Each of these items, while not a map in the narrow sense, does share important characteristics with a geographical map.

Opening up the discussion is useful, because it challenges children to explore these issues for themselves. Minerva's students made some very profound comments about the nature of symbolism, the use of graphic representation, and the distinction between the map and the thing mapped. The *Stuff That Works!* guide on *Signs, Symbols, and Codes* revisits mapping in this broader sense.

Graphing and Mapping

Many teachers and students see little if any distinction between a graph and a map. Both graphs and maps represent information using graphic devices and symbols; both can be used to present data from an investigation. Sometimes, there is a choice between the two. In fact, there are a lot of similarities, and in the broad meaning of *mapping,* a graph could be considered a kind of map. In diagram form, it shows the relationship between different kinds of data, such as plant growth and time. A map is also a diagram of relationships, such as the distribution of things in space or of a variable such as temperature in space.

A graph shows the relationships among two or more variables. These could be time and stock prices, number of classroom interruptions and person doing the interrupting, name of teacher and number of children in the class, percent of total budget and purpose of expenditure, etc. Bar and line graphs and pictograms use distance along each axis to represent the size or value of each variable. Pie graphs use an angle for the same purpose. In each case, a system of graphic devices stands for

some kind of relationship. The devices that are used include the length of a line, the position of a dot or an "x" on the page, the size of a figure, and the opening of an angle. Graphs are useful in showing the relationships between the variables.

A geographical map, by contrast, uses the two dimensions on the page to represent two or more dimensions of physical space. Geographical maps, at a minimum, show something about where things are. Many maps add a third variable by using a variety of graphic devices to indicate its value at different locations. These devices include color, symbols, cross-hatching, shading, contour lines, etc.

Graphing and mapping are obviously related, but they receive very different treatment in most curricula. Graphing is considered an essential topic in mathematics, and graphing skills are revisited repeatedly in the elementary, middle, and secondary grades. Students are expected both to interpret someone else's graphs and to construct their own. Maps, in contrast, are usually presented as part of social studies, typically in the secondary grades. Students may be expected to find countries, states, cities, and rivers on existing maps, or to copy data from existing maps. Map reading exercises

are not usually given much importance, particularly with the decline of geography as a separate school subject. Children are almost never asked to construct their own maps from their own data.

It's unfortunate that more weight isn't given to mapping in the schools. In many ways, a map is a more intuitive representation than a graph. Mapping deals with concrete, observable objects, such as furniture, streets, and stores, while graphs are more abstract. For this reason, some teachers who have done mapping activities in their classrooms have suggested that mapping be introduced as a pre-graphing activity.

For more advanced work, it is reasonable to ask whether a map or a graph is a better way to represent a set of data. As part of a teacher workshop, thermometers were taped at ten strategic locations around a large, drafty room. The teachers were divided into groups, and each group was asked to read all ten thermometers. They had to represent the data in a way that could reveal relationships and raise further questions about the heating and ventilation of the room.

One group made a line graph, shown in Figure 4-1. This graph shows the temperature at each station, but does not reveal the locations of the stations, nor the spatial temperature pattern in the room.

Another group made a map of the room showing the ten stations and added a bar graph displaying the temperature at each station, shown in Figure 4-2. In this case, all of the data is shown, but the map of locations is separate from the temperature data at each location. As a result, the relationship between location and temperature is still obscure.

A third group drew a map of the room and wrote the temperature at each thermometer location with the idea of drawing lines through points of equal temperature, as on a weather map. The problem was that they did not have enough identical readings to connect together into a temperature line, so they combined temperatures into groups of three degrees. Even so, they had to make several estimations as to where temperature lines should go. This group used different types of cross-hatching—a classic graphic device—to show the temperature distribution directly on the map. Their map is shown in Figure 4-3.

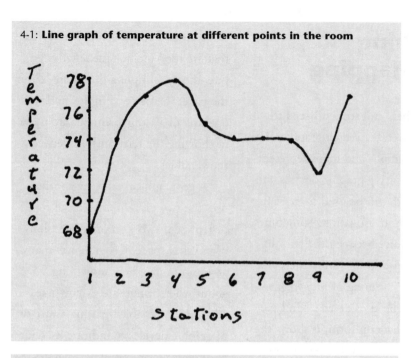

4-1: **Line graph of temperature at different points in the room**

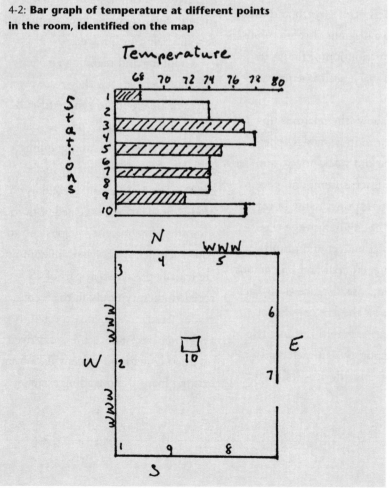

4-2: **Bar graph of temperature at different points in the room, identified on the map**

The map in Figure 4-3 was more successful than the graphs in Figures 4-1 and 4-2 in revealing relationships and raising further questions. A drafty region in the upper left corner was a result of a window that didn't close properly. A plume of warm air from the center to the upper right came from a radiator at the square central pillar. Some teachers raised the question, "Are there ways of tracing air movement to see if it really coincides with areas of equal temperature?"

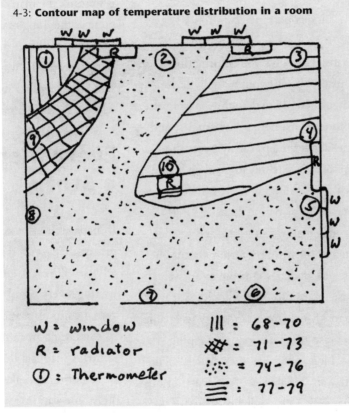

4-3: **Contour map of temperature distribution in a room**

W = window
R = radiator
T = Thermometer

||| = 68-70
✕ = 71-73
∴ = 74-76
≡ = 77-79

4-4: **Linda's map of a table in the science area**

Map of a table in The science center

Geographical Maps Show Where Things Are

Linda Crews teaches second grade at P.S. 84, on the Upper West Side of Manhattan. The school has long been a center for innovative programs, such as two-way bilingual Spanish-English, Primary Language Record (PLR), and inquiry science. Linda has considerable experience in PLR. She describes how she began a unit on mapping:

We started talking about maps today. I showed the class a few samples of maps including two I made of a table in the science area and my desk (Figure 4-4).

I explained that these were maps but did not go into any detail about what kind they were or the definition of "map." I asked them to look at the maps and tell me what they saw. Here are some of their responses:

Dinosaurs, books
Cups
Water
Places
The "What Is It?" box
Mealworms/beetles
Calendar

Guinea pig cage (because it looks like "Dirtball's" cage)

I then asked, "What kind of information do these maps give us?" They responded:

Where things are

What dinosaurs look like

How many things there are

I wanted some feedback on their responses pertaining to where things are or, actually, details on the kinds of things we could get from maps. So I started asking them questions like:

- How many books are on my desk?
- Where is one object in relation to another?
- Is there a stapler on my desk?

They responded by looking at the maps instead of running to my desk or looking at the table in the science area. Based on their answers, it was clear to me that they understood how to get information from maps and that a map could be a picture of many things in a room or at a place.

I then asked them to make a map of the table they sit at. My instructions were: "Draw a map of what you see at your table." The results all appear to be from an aerial view. I was pleased that the only question was, "Can I color it?"

Linda's narrative captures a key point about one of the purposes of maps. They give you information about a place without your actually having to go there. Like drawings, narratives, photographs, newspaper articles, and travelogues, maps can tell you about a remote place. Built into this purpose is a way of judging a map: Does it give me the information I am seeking? Linda's maps of her desk and science area fulfilled this criterion because her second graders were able to answer basic questions just by looking at the maps. More important, they were able to grasp this function of mapping.

Linda notes that most of her children drew an "aerial view." At the end of this chapter is an extended portrayal of Mary Flores' work with special education children. There you will see the activities Mary developed to help children represent collections of objects from a bird's-eye view.

This activity gets at some of the most basic ideas behind a geographical map. Every map (other than a fantasy map) is supposed to represent some big or little piece of the actual world. In other words, the map stands for the thing mapped. Lines, words, and symbols on the map represent real things. The key word here is "represents." A common mistake is to think the map can ever be the same as the thing mapped. It can't be, nor should it be. A map never shows things exactly the way they are, but only some aspects of reality that have been selected by the mapmaker.

Every Map Tells a Story

If maps are not perfect reflections of reality, then what can they possibly tell us? Like every story, every piece of writing, every bit of verbal or non-verbal communication, every map tells us something from the teller's viewpoint. A map is a form of communication, from mapmaker to map-reader. This observation applies to maps made by professional cartographers as well as those made by children. A road map, such as Figure 1-7 in Chapter 1, is designed to show you how to get from one place to another by car. It is a fairly accurate representation of the physical layout, except that the roads themselves and tourist attractions are usually drawn way out of proportion to their actual size. It may also be intended to impress you with how easy it is to get around, to advertise the many "places of interest" and "recreation areas," and to entice you to drive there for a visit. On the other hand, a bus map, such as Figure 1-8 of Chapter 1, emphasizes the places you can get to by mass transit, the ease of making connections between bus and bus or bus and subway. The bus map tells a story the New York City Transit Authority wishes to communicate.

Children's maps also reflect particular views of reality. The maps made by some of Felice Piggott's students demonstrate this point clearly. Felice teaches fifth grade at P.S. 145 in Manhattan Valley, a largely Hispanic community on Manhattan's Upper West Side. Most of her students live in the Valley, but some travel by subway from other neighborhoods in northern Manhattan. Over the past five years, Felice has developed a variety of ways of engaging her students in investigating their own local environment. She writes:

I have asked them to draw a map of "THE ROUTE TO SCHOOL." We discussed ways to do this—symbols, directions, start/finish, etc. Maps have come in from most everyone in the class, which generally means they liked doing it. Some are brilliant and some completely unreadable. Some are very baroque, while others are clear and direct.

We discussed maps that "made sense" to us—in that we were able to describe exactly the route that he or she took to school—from a wide assortment of the maps handed in. I would say that about half of the kids were able to depict clearly what route they took. Then we discussed AGAIN, why make a map? What kind of map do we need to travel by car, by train, on foot? Different maps are used for different tasks.

Figure 4-5 shows one of the maps from Felice's class. The mapmaker lives a few blocks from the school. The map shows the child's house, the school and two landmarks along the way: Booker T. Washington Junior High School (known in the neighborhood as "Booker T") and a favorite candy store. The most striking feature of the map consists of the boundaries. The map is bounded on three sides by parks (Riverside Park, Central Park, and Morningside Park) and on the fourth by a housing project (Frederick Douglass Houses). The parks are represented by trees and the housing project by buildings, all seen in side view and leaning into the map. She seems to be telling us that these are the boundaries of her world.

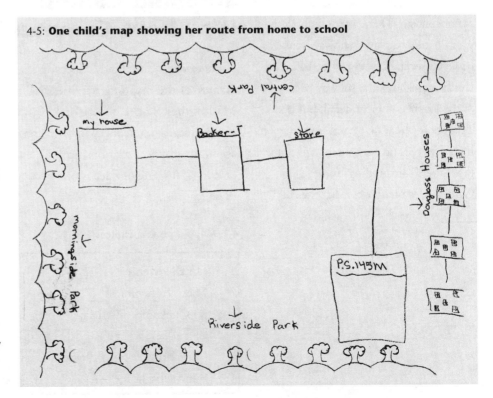

4-5: **One child's map showing her route from home to school**

Figure 4-6 shows a very different kind of route map. It was drawn by a student who commutes by subway from Washington Heights, about 70 blocks further uptown. The map is neither drawn to scale nor does it preserve directions. Nevertheless, it provides an accurate account of the daily trip to school, from the child's viewpoint. He walks from his home in the Roosevelt Gardens housing development to the 168th St. subway station. There he catches the local train, passing the 161st, 155th, 145th, 135th, 125th, 116th and 110th Street stations before getting off at 103rd St. The stations are shown accurately and in sequence—getting off at the right stop is clearly a major concern. Then, after climbing the prominently displayed subway steps, he walks several blocks to P.S. 145. This child's map shows the subway part of the journey in great detail, but is less clear about the walk to and from the train. There is no adornment except for the flowers surrounding Roosevelt Gardens. It's pretty clear that the child is happy to reach home each day.

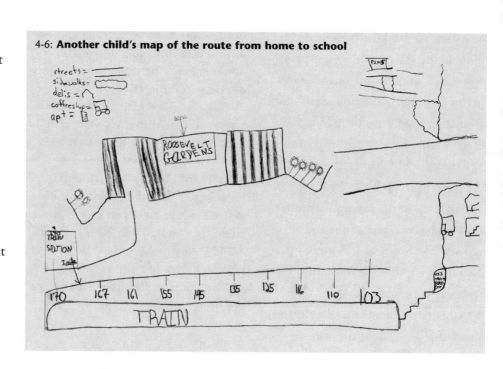

4-6: **Another child's map of the route from home to school**

Mapping Games: It's About Communication

Some teachers have used "Mapping Games" as pre-mapping activities. Most of these games involve oral communication, to convey information about the physical relationship of things. Angel Gonzalez is one of these teachers.

Angel Gonzalez is a science cluster teacher (specialist) at the Family School, a small public alternative school in Central Harlem, New York City. Angel has been an elementary teacher for about 15 years and has been engaged in teaching inquiry science during most of that time. As a cluster teacher, he has from second to fifth grade classes during their classroom teachers' prep periods.

4-7: **Mapping game choices**

> **On the Menu**
> I See Something
> 20 Questions on a Map
> Blind Tic-Tac-Toe
> Comparing Pattern Blocks
> Blind Checkers

Angel has made extensive use of mapping games with his second- and third-graders. He posts "On the Menu" (Figure 4-7) in his science lab, which lists all of the available mapping games. The children select the game they want and sit at the table that has the activity guide and supplies for that particular game. To play "I See Something," one child acts as leader. He or she picks an object in the room and describes it by saying, "I see something that…" and describing attributes of the object, such as shape, color, size, and location. The other children have to guess what the object is. The Activity Guide for "Twenty Questions on a Map" is shown in Figure 4-8. It is similar to "I See Something," except that the secret object is a place on a map rather than an actual thing in the room.

"Blind Tic-Tac-Toe" is one of several games in which the two players are separated by a cardboard screen that prevents them from seeing each other's desk space. Each player has a Tic-Tac-Toe board. The idea is to play the game by communicating moves orally. Each student uses his or her own board to keep track of the moves, but neither can look at the other's board. This game requires children to invent their own ways of describing locations on a three-by-three grid. "Blind Checkers" is similar, but more

4-8: Activity Guide for "Twenty Questions on a Map"

> **Twenty Questions on a Map**
>
> **Needs:**
> A large poster-size map or bigger
>
> **Tasks:**
> One person is the leader. The rest of the group may ask questions.
> The leader thinks of a place on the map. The others ask questions such as
>
> > Is it west of the Mississippi?
> > Is it smaller than New Jersey?
> > Does it have many lakes?
> > Are there mountains there?
>
> Everyone takes turns being the leader

demanding, because the grid is eight-by-eight and because both the starting and ending locations of each move are important.

Angel writes:

Kids like the 20 Questions game, and it helps to introduce lots of map concepts regarding directions (N, W, S, and E), latitude and longitude, right and left.

The "I See Something Game" is well enjoyed. Kids are forced to use language in describing attributes of a thing, such as color, shape, size, texture, location, etc. Most games require a good knowledge of left and right. So a good routine warm-up activity is "Simon Says," emphasizing use of right and left, hands and feet.

These games have two important uses. As Angel points out, they develop skill in observation, identifying things, describing locations, and orienting oneself, which are major aspects of drawing, mapping, and visual thinking. To have them focus on what they learned, Angel asked the students to write their reflections on these mapping games. One student's account of "Blind Tic-Tac-Toe" is shown in Figure 4-9.

At the same time, these games get at the problem of communicating about places. They emphasize how difficult it is to give place information using only words, because maps and other graphics are not allowed.

Maps Provide Directions

Not all maps are intended to give information about a place. There are some that have been designed to tell others how to get somewhere. These maps are like instruction manuals that tell the user how to get a job done. Adults make a map of this sort when they provide a route map showing how to get to one's house or a social function. Felice Piggott asked her fifth-grade students to make maps of this kind. (The assignment is described in more detail later.) One student's work is shown as Figure 4-10.

4-9: One student's reflections on "Blind Tic-Tac-Toe"

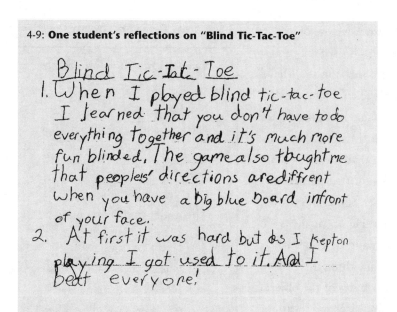

4-10: A map showing how to get to the computer

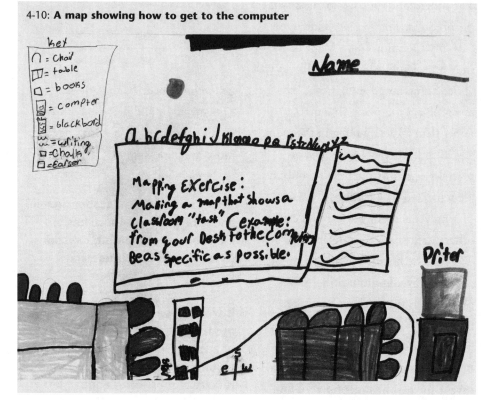

Note that the map includes the blackboard, which displays Felice's assignment to the class. Her directions included the following: "Your map MUST be able to be read by someone else and the task shown completed by them." This statement provided the children with a criterion for evaluating their maps.

It was more important to Felice that her students understood one another's maps than that she understood them. In fact, this criterion was contained in her directions. This activity—like Minerva's map scavenger hunt—also seemed to generate a great deal of excitement and effort by the children. It demonstrates again that children can find mapping to be a very powerful and engaging form of communication.

Mapping in a First-Grade Classroom

Beginning with Piaget, considerable research has been done on how children understand maps. Based on his own experiments, Piaget concluded that children younger than about seven are generally unable to construct maps from more than one point of view (their own) or even to read maps constructed from another point of view. (See Chapter 2.)

Sketching a Chalk Box from "Aerial" and "Chin" Views

Annette Purnell, a first-grade teacher at C.E.S. 42 in the South Bronx, did some informal research of her own that seems to refute Piaget's conclusions. Initially, she worked with only six of her students—those who have the most difficulty in the whole-class group. She was able to do this work while the other children were pulled out for other programs. She began by rehearsing numbers and directions with them. These were actually elementary experiences with a simple coordinate system.

Our first mapping inquiry took place in our classroom. The six boys were asked to stand on the "perimeter of the rug." Once they were there, I took the opportunity to channel their bounding energy and restlessness and practice one-to-one correspondence from math: "Take two steps in; take two more steps in. Take three steps out. Walk four back in, etc." In the center of the rug was a box of blackboard chalk. (See Figure 4-11.) I asked them to describe what they saw.

4-11: **Looking at a chalk box from an aerial view**

4-12: **Looking at a chalk box from a "chin" view**

JAMES:
We're looking down on the box.
We are up on top.

LONNIE:
It's square.

Next, I asked them to put their chins on the floor and tell what they saw. (See Figure 4-12.)

The delightful effects here turned out to be a result of the printing on the box. We did a "go round" where each child shifted position to another side of the box. The shape is now similar—it is still a rectangle—but the size is different, and the print is now upside-down on the new side of the box. Some of the children say "12 upside-down," while others don't. Could you ask for anything better?

Can You Find My Desk?

Next, I asked them to map items on their desks. What luck! To my surprise, each child's desk arrangement was slightly different.

Differences among the six desks:
- Notebook, pencil to its right
- Notebook, no pencil
- Notebook, pencil on top, to the left
- Open notebook, pencil in spine
- Notebook, pencil laying across it, perpendicularly
- Notebook, pencil case and 3 pencils to its left

4-13: **Observing and mapping desktops**

The children were asked if they wished to map their desk spaces standing on a chair for an "aerial" view, or sitting on their chairs and looking from a "chin" view. They chose "standing on the chair" (and having it sanctioned), naturally! (See Figure 4-13.)

Playground to Chalk Box to Playground

One child had decals on his note-book. There were also prominent decals on his map, but they were misplaced. When I asked him where the decals were on his notebook, he pointed to them. I asked him to look at the decals on his map, and asked if he'd like to put them where they were on his notebook. He erased them and replaced them in the proper places. This was the only intervention I made.

I asked them if they would like to invite their friends in, before lunch, to use their new maps to find which child's table was which. They chose girls, by and large. The "map readers" had a difficult time locating their "find." I had to scaffold them, and help them use a process of elimination to get through the activity. To my surprise, one girl was getting visibly frustrated.

Annette felt in retrospect that the children weren't adequately prepared for the map-reading task. The "map readers" had not been involved in the initial activities on drawing the chalk box or mapping desktops. She felt that she needed to structure mapping experiences for the whole class. The children's interest in the playground provided an opportunity.

In reflecting, I see that map-reading is an observation process in and of itself. It was harder than I thought it would be, because the clues were subtle and the maps were the only indication they had about which desk to look for.

A week has passed, and I want to get the whole class involved in mapping. They have just come in from playing outside. There are painted dinosaur footprints on our yard's ground, which are new this year. The playground apparatus is familiar to these first-graders. I began by asking, "What shapes do you remember seeing in the play-ground?" We named them without writing them down. Afterwards, I gave them paper, pencils, and note-books to lean on. Then we went outside to make the maps.

Two days later, the children paired off with partners of their choice and shared their playground maps with each other. They listened

to one another and seemed to enjoy the task. I collected the papers and praised them on their collective work and work habits.

Annette will return to the play-ground activity shortly, but in the meantime, she revisits the chalk box activity. Some of the children have developed the ability to predict what the box will look like from different points of view.

Another week has passed, and I have the six boys again. We revisit the original activity to get verbal responses this time. This group is also practicing taking turns and listening to each other's responses.

The children stand at various points around a chalk box on the floor. Each child takes a turn report-ing what he sees. Without moving, they go through this exercise three times. Here are their responses:

	First Go-Round	Second Go-Round	Third Go-Round
James	I see "21" and words and squiggles	I see circles that squiggle and chalk	I see two sides are longer and two sides are shorter
Jared	I see a little blue circle	I see a 12	I see the word "chalk"
Pedro	I see a blue triangle	I see a little blue circle	I see upside down "chalk"
Giancarlo	I see "chalk"	I see a box that has a triangle	I see little white squiggly things
Lonnie	I see a blue line	I see a triangle	I see that circle
Darren	I see orange	I see white things	I see a blue circle

We stand on the perimeter of the rug and do some more stepping into and out of the area through a calling out of steps. This is also to give ideas about how to give directions during future mapping activities. I tell them that they will be drawing what they see from both "aerial" and "chin" views.

I take one child directly over the box and talk about an aerial view again. While looking down from a standing position, one child (James) said he knew how and where to stand so that he would see the words upside-down. He moved to an opposite position. He tested his hypothesis and it worked! Another child (Lonnie) said he could do it too. He went over two spaces, and saw basically the same view. He smiled and noted that he was wrong. He moved again until it was upside-down. This led into our three go-rounds in telling what we saw. Each child stayed in the same position through all three go-rounds, and all views are "aerial."

Annette wanted to revisit the playground as well. Two things would be different this time:

- They had already tried it once; and
- The first time they had only discussed the shapes beforehand; this time she would also list and draw them, before they went outside.

Annette wanted to know whether and how these two rather subtle interventions would affect the quality of their maps. She was pleasantly surprised by the outcome! In her words:

Before the whole class (28 children) revisited the playground, we discussed and listed the playground shapes from memory. This time I drew and wrote the words. Where children named triangles, I gave several views and told them so. Where they mentioned lines and shapes that had several views, I drew them to allow and encourage different entry points.

We went in the afternoon. The playground was again empty. All made drawings except one. This child does well in the group of six, but thus far refuses to stay prepared in the larger group. The children spent the same amount of time, but I see much more detail in their drawings.

Jarod's and Bryant's drawings illustrate Annette's point about seeing more detail. A photo of the playground is shown in Figure 4-14. Note the circular structure to the left, the triangle in the center and the box-shaped structure with the rounded roof on the right. In the foreground, there are dinosaur footprints that are not visible in the photo.

4-14: **Photograph of the playground**

4-15: **Jarod's first drawing of the playground**

4-16: **Jarod's second drawing of the playground**

4-17: **Bryant's first drawing of the playground**

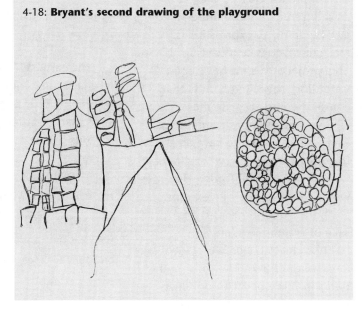
4-18: **Bryant's second drawing of the playground**

In Jarod's first drawing, (Figure 4-15) the triangular structure, on the left side, can be made out clearly. The structure on the right may correspond with the box. His second drawing (Figure 4-16) shows the triangular structure clearly in the middle ground and the rounded box to its right and in front of it. The dinosaur footprints are in the foreground. Between the first and second attempts, Jarod is developing what Piaget called "logical correspondence." To a much greater extent, the objects on the map correspond with the objects being mapped.

Bryant's two drawings show a similar kind of progression. In the first (Figure 4-17), all three structures are present, but the triangle is to the right rather than in the middle. His second drawing (Figure 4-18) shows the triangle in the middle. Piaget described the correct ordering of mapped objects as "topological correspondence."

Mapping in a Fifth-Grade Class

Annette's work demonstrates that young children can develop logical and topological correspondence and an understanding of different points of view. She provided minimal, but very strategic, intervention, dealt with objects and places that were already familiar to the children, and gently guided them towards a greater understanding. She concludes her account with the following reflections:

I enjoy watching a project unfold as children gain more understanding, and by doing so express ideas, make discoveries, and develop abilities. This project thus far has begun unfolding, revealing results that charm me and surprise me.

I've seen two basic unfoldings. First, children seem to have an affinity for this kind of work, where there was no previous indication that they would. Second, their inventions are born through necessity, for the sake of communication.

Two children who are academically at extremes now show convergent paths in this work. Through mapping, I first noticed the similarities in their approach to the recording of observations. Both showed a level of detail that others did not include.

Felice Piggott teaches fifth grade at P.S. 145 on West 105th Street in New York City. Felice has "traveled up" with this class. Most of the children were with her last year, some for two years. Felice presents a picture of mapping, not as a unit that covers a week or two, but as an activity to which children repeatedly return throughout the year. We will see how skills developed during the fall provide the groundwork for a redesign project in the spring. Throughout this account you will read terms such as "cardinal directions," "scale," and "perspective." A more systematic treatment of these topics follows Michael Gatton's account of mapping work in a middle school, later in this chapter.

Map of Your Room

Felice begins mapping when the children return to school in September.

The early stuff that we've done is what I call "orientation chores"— a "Map of Your Room" is first-week stuff that helps me get to know my kids better.

Mapping is a great way to start the school year. Maps of places that are "your own" are excellent vehicles for children to get to know each other, and for the teacher to get a sense of who they are.

After they do that I post the maps and have students discuss what they see in each other's maps.

- Are they all the same? Some use crayon, some pencil.
- Do they all look at it from the same view?
- From this we get discussions of perspective and use of symbols.

Felice and her children talk. The classroom is filled with talk. As they compare the maps posted around

the room, they notice that they don't come from the same view. They are drawn from different perspectives. Some things are drawn from "straight on"—the human perspective. Others are drawn from the top—a bird's-eye view.

After discussing their own room maps, the talk ranges to other maps they know: maps of the United States, the subway. Felice takes out some maps to prompt the conversation. The children talk about the size of the map, the size of the thing mapped. As they wonder about the differences between the map of the subway and the map of the United States, they begin to think about how the same thing may be drawn in different sizes. Such ponderings are the backdrop for beginning to think about scale.

Felice holds maps of New York City and the subway upside-down or sideways, to raise initial ideas about orientation. Symbols and keys come into the conversation as Felice points them out. The stage is set for more mapping.

Mapping Your Room Revisited

After that I ask kids to redo their maps using any or all of the map-making tools we have discussed. We then repeat the posting/discussion process using old and new maps and comparing them.

Felice posts each child's maps side-by-side to make comparisons easy. Natalie's second map (Figure 4-20) shows the influence of class conversations since the first maps were done. In the first map (Figure 4-19) there is a combination of perspectives. The desk is drawn from directly above (plan view). The chest is shown as it would be seen from the middle of the ceiling looking down obliquely. The door, closet and filing cabinet are drawn from the side (side elevation).

In the second map of her room, Natalie consistently constructs a side elevation. Is it a "better" map? In terms of helping us orient ourselves in her room, the answer is probably "no," but that misses the developmental issue. Natalie was given some ideas about ways to represent a space, and she is playing with them. In the second map she has also incorporated a key. The symbols she uses for knobs, wheels, handles, and antenna are the same shapes she used to represent these things in the first map. She is beginning to construct a key that serves as a guide to her symbols.

4-19: **Natalie's first map of her room**

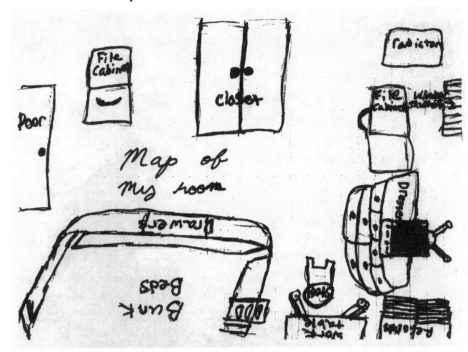

4-20: **Natalie's second map of her room**

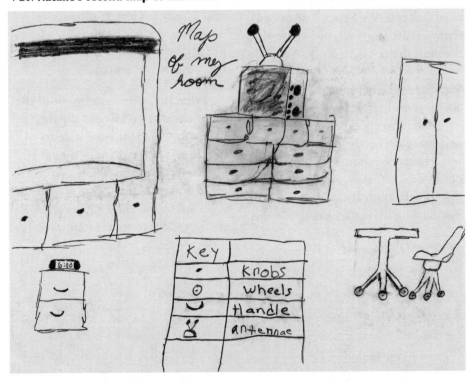

Map Your Route to School

Two weeks pass before Felice returns to mapping with the activity described below. They haven't really left mapping, though. Many of the maps are left on the walls. Children look at the ways others have drawn their rooms, what they have in them, and they discuss maps.

I have asked them to draw a map of the "Route to School." Previous to this assignment, we discussed ways to do this—symbols, directions, start / finish, etc. Three days later, maps of the route to school have come in from most everyone in the class, which generally means they liked doing it. We haven't discussed them yet (tomorrow), but I've looked through them. Some are brilliant and some completely unreadable. Some are very baroque, while others are clear and direct.

I will have children look at them and compare each other's maps. We will discuss commonalties and differences. We will look for maps that clearly illustrate a "route" and discuss why they are successful maps.

With this assignment Felice introduces maps as being purposeful: they are meant to communicate. As they talk about how to do the map, the children raise questions: "Do I have to draw all the buildings I pass?"

"What about streets and signs?" Felice reminds them of symbols as a way to simplify drawing. A key is needed as a sort of dictionary of the symbols they use.

Felice sets up the discussion so that one child would study a classmate's map, and then give a narrative of how the classmate went from home to school. The mapmaker confirmed (or rejected) the narrative.

The next day we discussed maps that "made sense" to us in that we were able to describe exactly the route that he or she took to school.

STANSKI
(TALKING OF NATALIE'S MAP):
I don't understand it at all, but I don't take the bus.

MIOSHA:
I do and I understand.

From the wide assortment of the maps handed in, I would say that about half the kids were able to depict clearly what route they took. Then we discussed AGAIN "Why make a map?" What kind of map do we need to travel by car, by train, on foot? Different maps are used for different tasks.

Natalie's map (Figure 4-21) includes a compass rose, but it is no more than a circle with letters, N for north being at the top. She has not yet understood the connections among the directions in the real world, their relative positions on the map, and the directions indicated by the compass rose. Felice introduced the idea of a compass rose when the class was looking at published maps. It will take time for students to understand these relatively abstract relationships.

A week has passed, but mapping remains present: the home-to-school maps are still posted on the walls. Kids go back to them, figure them out, and announce: "Hey, I know what Miosha means here."

4-21: **Natalie's map of her route to school**

Route to a Destination within the Classroom

Next assignment: Using our classroom, draw the route for a particular task to be done from your desk to a destination in our room (from your desk to water fountain, for example). Use "Start" and "End" and cardinal directions. Your map must be able to be read by someone else and the task shown completed by him or her. Write a narrative of your path on the back.

They talked a lot about this assignment before they began. "Do I have to show everything in the classroom?" "Can I just show my desk and where I'm going to?"

Felice usually will not answer this sort of question directly. She may turn it back to the child in a more manageable form, or she may simply leave it with him to think about. In this case

she talked the class through an example: the path from her desk to the fish tank. They talked of landmarks that would help orient the map-reader: the rug, the rocking chair, the computer tables. They talked of the use of cardinal directions as an easy way to indicate which way you turn. By this time the class was using cardinal directions consistently.

Some kids have trouble making the map: Should I draw the whole room? Do I have to include a drawing of each kid at his or her desk? Others draw it easily from their perspective but have trouble using a compass rose or giving cardinal directions. Some kids draw only the path needed to complete the task while others draw the entire classroom and use a dotted line to show where to go.

The maps ranged from the whimsical drawing of Pedro to the relatively well-proportioned map of Juan. The directions, too, differed in clarity. Pedro (Figure 4-22) gave directions along his path: "Go south . . . continue . . . turn east (you can't go over a desk!) . . .Go south . . . 'I made it!'" Juan (Figure 4-23) was more explicit.

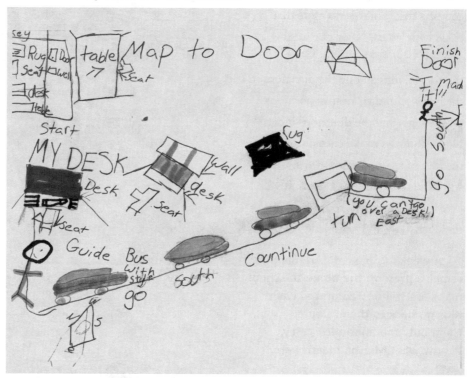

4-22: **Pedro's map from his desk to the door**

4-23a: **Juan's map**

4-23b: **Juan's directions**

first walk 3 steps east then turn North east then walk 6 steps turn North walk 8 steps turn east walk 8 steps. your at the goal

Some kids made maps that made sense to each other, but made no sense to me. A few kids didn't finish, either because they never do, or because they were VERY COMPULSIVE about detail.

Three days later, following another's map:

Very interesting to watch them hand over their maps to their class-mates and either walk behind them silently or narrate every step of the way because their map lacks cardinal directions or a point of orientation.

Some kids wanted to do a larger map showing a task within the school (from our room to the office) and wondered how they would be able to show it. One kid (see Juan, Figure 4-23) was counting steps involved in his task and noted them on his directions. This made me think that perhaps SCALE was an important target for the next exercise and that I would "section off" an area of the classroom for them to map using floor tiles as a guide.

Generally the kids enjoy the mapping exercises and appear to look forward to them, but for many of them it's a really challenging task. More time was needed for sharing by the whole group. Sharing occurred with the small groups working together, but whole class sharing is also needed. I think we should have walked through a few more "dry runs" before we committed to paper. Some kids were very confused about direction and perspective. About one quarter of the class really nailed this activity. Most still need more map-making experience.

The understanding of scale requires abstract thinking and, specifically, proportional thinking. Felice's fifth graders are at the very beginning of developing this understanding. In the next section we consider this development more thoroughly.

Constructing a Master Map: Establishing Scale

The previous week Felice saw in the work of Juan and a few others an invitation to move on to constructing maps to scale. Now she pursues this direction.

Review the previous student-made maps:

- **Which maps communicate better than others? Why?**
- **Which maps show an accurate representation of relative size (are the desks the same sizes?)**
- **Which maps do not communicate effectively? Why?**

At this point the children have experience to draw upon. They have made maps of their rooms, the route from home to school, and the map of a task within the classroom. They have become good at commenting on one another's ideas and work. A classroom culture has developed that routinely includes serious, supportive talk.

Another aspect of the culture is that work is always in progress and exists on many interconnected fronts. Children expect to go back and look again, critically, at what they have done. They also expect to draw upon much of what they know.

I asked the students:

- **How could we more accurately portray our classroom?**
- **How could we show sizes of objects in relation to each other?**
- **How do mapmakers do it?**

Once I elicited a sense of scale or proportion, I introduced the concept of floor tiles as the unit to measure the room and elicited ways of using them in our "scale."

Children see that the desks should be the same size on the map, since they are the same size in the room. The same is true for chairs. Then they see that the amount of floor they cover should be the same.

Using the floor tiles (12"square) as the "norm" and a LARGE sheet of graph paper, we focused on a small portion of the room (the rug) and used an initial scale of 1:1 (meaning one floor tile to one box on the graph paper sheet) to "map" it. After using that initial scale to map the rug, we realized that when we would attempt to map out the classroom, we would need a VERY LARGE sheet of paper.

Children have had experience in using arbitrary units of measure. For the purpose of mapping the classroom, the floor tile is an excellent unit. Typically it is thought of as a unit of length, not area. Thus, a desk is four tiles long and three tiles wide. The notion of it being twelve tiles in area is somewhat more difficult.

We tried scales of 4:1 and 3:1 before we decided on 2:1. So we then revised the scale to 2:1 (2 floor tiles = 1 graph paper square). We then used 2:1 to map out a small area for the MASTER MAP.

Felice encourages experimentation. Children come up with ideas, try them out, and make judgments about the results. The scale of 2:1 is not obviously better than a scale of 1:1 or 3:1 or 4:1 as long as the class is only talking abstractly. When they see what it looks like, there is a basis for judgment. At the end of the activity Felice made these observations:

Children with weak division and fraction concepts needed visual/hands-on experience— it was important to keep them engaged. I wanted to do more than a small section of the classroom, but it took kids a while to grasp this concept. Trying to do more than to introduce SCALE in this lesson would have been inappropriate. Doing the section of the MASTER MAP together was enough.

Felice extended the experience with different scales by asking:

- Which scale is more appropriate to map a large space?
- Which would be better for a small space?

Mapping with a Master Map: Our Desks as the Parts of a Whole

A week has passed since the initial work with scale. Felice has made a large MASTER MAP that is posted on the front wall. Its presence keeps mapping alive in the room during the week when no additional mapping was done. The plan is for children to map their desks to the same 2:1 scale, then place them on the MASTER MAP. Approximately two periods (80 minutes) were scheduled for this work.

We reviewed our work from last week; we discussed our scale (2 to 1) and how it would translate to paper. We decided we would work in teams of four (basically how many are seated in a desk grouping):

1. Show your group's desk grouping (with or without chairs) to SCALE on your paper.
2. Place your desk in the appropriate area of the MASTER MAP of our classroom.

What happened? MONDO QUESTIONS?! Although we had agreed on a scale and had discussed and used it, kids were VERY uneasy about tackling the desks on their own. If they counted floor tiles on their own and came up with a number, I had to recount and tell them they were correct. Others were unsure of how to convert odd numbers of floor tiles to the scale and had to be talked through it. However, two teams had no trouble mapping their space.

I wondered about the children who had difficulty with this activity— was it purely mathematical or are they unable to comprehend Euclidean concepts of mapping/representation?

We did not have time to place desks on the MASTER MAP; after kids finished and we toured each team's work, the time was gone.

Mapping with a Master Map: Putting It All Together

Nearly three weeks pass before there is time to return to the classroom-mapping project. The goal is to complete the classroom map. One hour is available for this work:

- Re-introduce MASTER MAP and review scale.
- Give students opportunity to review their maps of "desk area" previously done.

- Task is to:
  - Cut out desk area maps;
  - Place on MASTER MAP (everyone in group must agree as to placement); and
  - Add missing elements (rugs, bookcases, closets, etc.) also to scale of MASTER MAP.

Felice's children are beginning to understand scale. Through this activity they will understand scale better. They will have a feel for the proportional representation that results from drawing to scale.

What happened? SO, SO INTER-ESTING!!! During the first part of the task some children realized that their "desk area" maps could not be accurate because they were much larger or smaller than other elements shown. (My desk was the only furniture shown in the MASTER MAP.) So then they feverishly revised their maps. Or, during the second part of the task (placing desk map on the MASTER MAP), children were not able to orient themselves without another group's desk map placed first. In other words they could only orient themselves in relation to someone or something else that belonged nearby in the classroom.

What the children do not understand is the use of coordinates. They don't know how to use the grid of the floor tiles as a coordinate system. Thus they can't locate their own desks except by using the locations of neighboring desks.

Questions and comments by kids:

NATALIE:
How do you show 1/2 of 1/2?

CAMILLE:
I never realized we had so many things in our room.

PEDRO:
Can we do the cafeteria next?

SYLVIE:
You know, now that I look at it – we all worked separately in groups to make this, but using scale made it all come together nice.

Using Maps as Tools for Redesign

Felice's kids finished their work on the classroom map before Thanksgiving. Felice was thinking about possible extensions. She wanted to incorporate mapping as part of a larger design/ redesign project. As Felice recounts the beginnings:

The kids were looking to continue mapping and had suggested that a large space would be challenging. We chose the cafeteria. Mapping and then analyzing the activities within the space seemed a natural progression. Since NONE of the humans in P.S. 145 like the current operations in the cafeteria, it seemed an apt site. Kids were very excited by the fact that something could possibly be changed through some action of theirs! They were quite eager to do this.

The initial talk of redesigning the cafeteria was in December. They

brainstormed the tasks ahead: observe how the cafeteria is laid out, collect data on cafeteria use, analyze data, and redesign the cafeteria. It was a month later when the project was picked up again.

January 14. Sum up where we left off 12/10/97 and refresh memory regarding scale. Discuss what we should do when we go to the cafeteria:
- **count tiles for the length and width**
- **draw shape of the room**
- **count tables**
- **show arrangement and features (columns, etc.).**

Divide up into "TEAMS": Garbage, Food Service, Research, Seating, Arrangements, and Traffic. Go to cafeteria.

We came back to our room and discussed what we drew/counted. The use of the previous scale was agreed on and we did the math for our basic room outline.

I was very pleased by how seriously they got their tasks in the cafeteria done! The math aspects were easier this time for scale and assembling the basic room outline was done fairly quickly. They are eager to go on!

Go on they did, through much of the spring semester. Redesigning the cafeteria became a thread that was picked up, set aside as other curricular demands took precedence, and picked up again, like coming back to an old friend. The full story of this part of Felice's year is told in the *Stuff That Works!* guide, *Designed Environments.*

Mapping in Middle School

Michael Gatton teaches biology in Intermediate School 143. He is expected to "cover" a curriculum with many topics. Thus it is harder for him than it is for elementary teachers to add topics to his course of study. He was able to try out some ideas in mapping because he figured out how to integrate mapping into the study of the cell. Mapping could lead to a clearer understanding of diffusion.

Michael introduced mapping ideas with "Desk Maps" and "Mapping a Classroom" (Activities 14 and 21 in Chapter 3) and "Locating Ourselves in Space" described below under Mapping Concepts. The two diffusion activities, diffusion of food coloring in water and diffusion of a scent in air, show how data can be recorded on a map.

Mapping Diffusion in a Petri Dish

"Mapping Diffusion in a Petri Dish" requires little in the way of mapping skills beyond making one-to-one correspondences. It is presented as Activity 22 in Chapter 3. Michael describes it as follows.

The activity used petri dishes and popsicle sticks, but as the activity progressed, my students suggested a better method. The popsicle sticks were used to make a rough ruler with zero at the center point.

The popsicle stick was then placed on top of a petri dish containing water. A drop of food coloring was placed in the water at the zero point and we used the ruler to measure the diffusion of the food coloring. If done properly, the results were something like the example below. (See Figure 4-24.)

My students came up with an improvement that involved drawing the ruler on a sheet of paper, then placing the petri dish on top of the ruler they had drawn. Among other advantages, this eliminated the possibility that students might accidentally drop the ruler into the petri dish during the activity.

4-24: Diffusion of food coloring in water

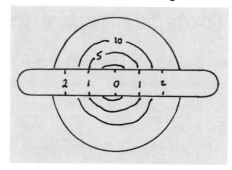

4-25: Javier's map of diffusion of food coloring in a petri dish

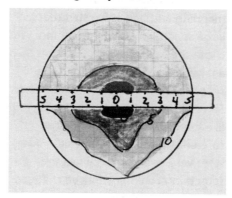

After placing the drop of food coloring, the children recorded the size of the drop on the duplicate map. They drew an outline of the spreading drop at five-minute intervals, filling in the space with color of the same intensity as the spreading drop. Javier's map of diffusion in a petri dish is shown in figure 4-25.

As a follow-up to the petri dish map, we transferred student maps to the chalkboard. I asked six students to put things on the board. Students were selected because either their maps were good representations of diffusion or because their tables were clearly bumped in the mapping process. (See Figure 4-26)

I did not tell students which maps best represented diffusion. Instead they were asked to pick and defend their answers. When I asked which samples looked like they had been bumped or accidentally moved during the activity, students almost unanimously picked samples that looked like the drawing to the right in 4-26. If the food coloring moved because the table was bumped, does that represent diffusion? Why not? We went back over what we know about diffusion, particularly the point that diffusion happens without the addition of energy to the system. When a table is bumped, energy is added to the system and the energy from the bump causes motion.

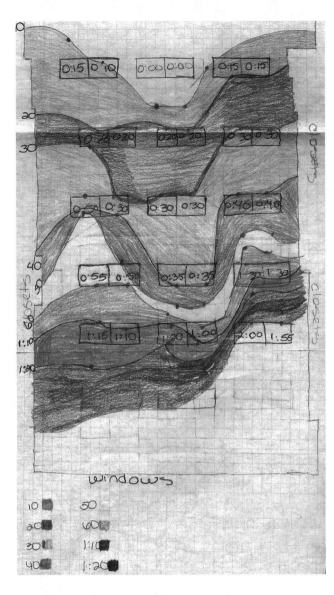

4-26: **Maps of calm diffusion (top) and disurbed diffusion (bottom)**

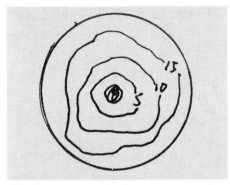

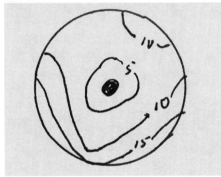

4-27: **Dora's map of the diffusion of a gas through the classroom**

Mapping Diffusion of Gas in a Classroom

In preparation for "Diffusion of a Gas in the Classroom," Michael's class spent two days in actually making a map of the classroom on which they would record the diffusion data. His journal entry reflects on this and describes the class work.

In retrospect, I believe that this activity of actually making a map was probably inappropriate. It was a time-consuming effort that in itself shed no light on diffusion. At the very least, a simplified map that depicted the classroom as a perfect rectangle would have done the job with no real need to draw all the corners and shelves and so on

within the room. The spacing of the desks was an essential component that also should have been included. The windows and doors could simply have been labeled so that the flow of air, even through the cracks of shut doors and windows might have been used to explain some of the data.

In the front of the room on the teacher's demonstration table, a bottle of potent air freshener was opened. I immediately began counting out five-second intervals. Students had been instructed to write down the time as soon as they smelled the air freshener. When (almost) everyone had smelled the

substance, we placed the times on our maps and then we drew contour lines (most of the students had experience with contour maps from studying weather in grade 7 with me) and colored the area in between. The map looked something like a weather map.

They drew a line through the desks where the odor was smelled in 10 seconds, another line through the desks where the odor was smelled in 20 seconds, and so on with lines for 30, 40, and 50 seconds. Dora's map for the spread of air freshener through the classroom air is seen in Figure 4-27.

Basic Mapping Concepts

Identifying the Concepts

Angel Gonzalez asked two of his fifth-grade classes what they knew about mapping. Here are some of their answers:

Maps help us find our way.

Some have grids.

Maps tell where places are.

They show routes of trains and buses.

Colors are used for codes.

Maps show miles.

Maps help us find our way.

They have compasses on them.

There are different kinds of maps such as for trains, the zoo, treasure, and blueprints.

The "what do we know about . . ." question taps what the most knowledgeable/vocal of students have been exposed to. The rough "map" it provides should not be confused with children's useable knowledge. Angel got a better picture of the level of knowledge in the class by asking the children for questions they had about mapping. What they saw as gaps in their knowledge or ability ranged from the basic to the very complex, even philosophical:

How do we read maps?

What are cardinal directions?

How to tell distances?

How are borders of places decided?

How do they know where to put the roads?

How did maps become an idea?

As children develop the abilities described they will be able to address many of the questions they have. These are the major concepts and abilities to develop.

- Point of view/perspective
- Orientation, cardinal directions, and the compass rose
- Symbols and keys
- Grids and scale

Point of View/Perspective

Children hear the assignment to map in different ways. In Felice's class, Karina interpreted the assignment to map her room as an invitation to list, pictorially, all the things in her room. The result is a logical map of her room. The things in the room are shown on the map. The spatial positioning of objects in the map, however, has little correspondence to their relative positions in the room.

Karina's initial map (see Figure 4-28) had other goals than to give a layout of her room. However, with most children (and later with Karina), we see a struggle to represent things in the same arrangement as they are really in. This is the complicated task of taking the real world and showing it on paper. As children draw their initial maps they first use one perspective, then another. Adults new to mapping do the same thing. Usually what we see is a mix of perspectives including top views, side views, and an occasional oblique view. Jeanette's first mapping of her own room (see Figure 4-29) is an example of a map that shows a mixed point of view: some objects are seen from the top while others are seen from the side. Things that Jeanette typically sees from the front, such as her dresser, the windows, and the walls, are shown in a side view, while the bed is shown in top view.

4-28: **Karina's first map of her room**

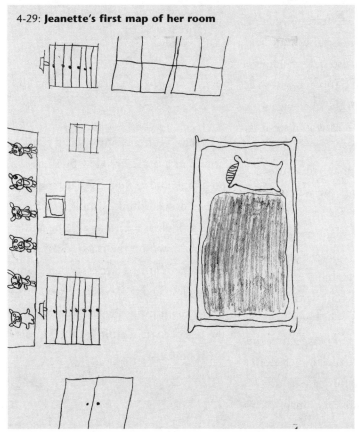

4-29: **Jeanette's first map of her room**

Jeanette's mix of perspectives is common in initial attempts at mapping. Maps of buildings on a street often include top views of streets and sidewalks and side views of the buildings. When a child looks around her room, some objects are seen primarily from a top view while others are almost always seen from the side.

Children can be challenged to adopt a point of view that, to cartographers, is more consistent—namely the top, or plan, view. Angel stood on a desk and looked down to introduce the notion of a "bird's-eye view." Felice had children compare their initial maps in terms of perspective. Questions such as "How much of the floor does your dresser cover?" may also help children see the usefulness of a top view. Jeanette's response to the challenge to draw her room as a bird would see it is shown in Figure 4-30.

Jeanette's earlier map with mixed perspectives represents the way she initially tried to draw what she saw. No inferences should be made about developmental issues, for what we are looking at is not so much ability as a lack of knowledge of different ways to represent things. When Felice and her class discussed issues of perspective, the idea of a "bird's-eye" view of her room became a possibility for Jeanette to consider as she planned her map.

4-30: **Jeanette's "birds-eye view" of her room**

Angel Gonzalez introduced the notion of a bird's-eye view by standing on a desk and asking, "What kind of shapes do you think I would see if I were as high as a bird or a plane and looking down on the classroom?" The children identified circles, squares, and rectangles. The task was to draw a map of the room using shapes, seen from the perspective of a bird at the top of the room.

The ability to take another point of view varies among fifth-graders. When Kathy placed herself at the ceiling, she saw the overhead fluorescent lights as foreground, blocking much of the floor space that was to be mapped. (See Figure 4-31.)

Orientation, Cardinal Directions, and the Compass Rose

To use a map (or just to make sense of it) you need to relate it to the space it represents. Children orient the map to the real space by relating landmarks in the map to corresponding landmarks in the real space. Children also orient the map by placing the north side of the map toward the north. Relating north on a map to a geographic north requires that:

- North is actually represented on the map, and
- The map-reader is able to identify the geographic north.

Providing landmarks and establishing the direction of north are two ways to help people make sense of a map. To line up a map with the space it represents, place the map on a horizontal surface so that objects shown on the right of the map lie to your right and

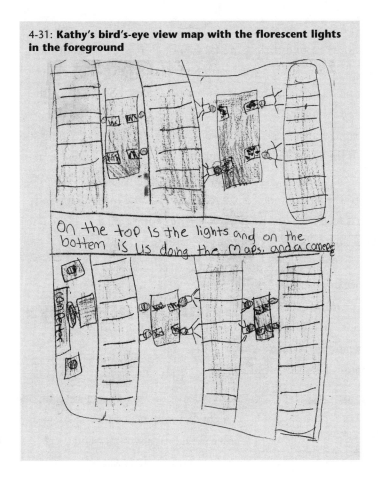

4-31: **Kathy's bird's-eye view map with the florescent lights in the foreground**

objects on the left of the map lie to your left. The result of this is that things straight ahead of you are at the top of the map, things behind you lie to the bottom. Children orient a map to a space when they place a classroom map so that the side of the map with the windows is nearer the real windows and the side with the coat closet is nearer the coat closet.

When children post their classroom maps on the walls, often it is without respect to the orientation of the actual classroom. The result is that things

lying on the right side of the map may actually lie to your right, but they also may lie to your left or behind you. Classroom maps are easiest to read if you follow this rule: rotate the map so the side of the map where wall "A" is drawn is at the top when the map is posted on wall "A." When maps are posted in other orientations, they are much harder to read. Reconciling such maps to the classroom is a good exercise in identifying landmarks and correlating them to classroom features. This is a way children learn to orient a map to the space it represents. Such orientation allows children to find their location on the map.

Indicating north on a map is a more complex process than providing landmarks to orient the map. You have to:

- establish north in the space you have mapped,
- orient the map to the space, and
- draw the compass rose with north in the same direction as in the space.

Angel Gonzalez began by asking children to point to the north. They pointed in all directions, including up. Angel asked for explanations. Here are examples of the responses he got:

The top of the map is north.

Mrs. D. said that north is toward the chalkboard.

Angel reminded them of the book *Follow the Drinking Gourd* in which escaping slaves used the Big Dipper to locate the North Star. Keeping a northward bearing was vital to survival. Angel presented the compass as an alternative to the North Star. Each child held his compass very still, then turned the compass until the letter "N" rested under the arrow. The compass face was then copied on the map as the compass rose. For the compass rose to be accurate in pointing to north on the map, it is essential that the map on which the compass rose is placed be carefully aligned with the area represented.

There are other ways to establish north than by using a compass or the North Star. Classes with a view of the noonday sun can establish north as the direction opposite the direction towards the sun. A more careful way of using sun and shadows to establish the direction of north is to record the shadows of a vertical rod at ten-minute intervals around midday. The shortest shadow is the one that points straight north.

Symbols and Keys

Symbols and keys are standard parts of maps. Social studies materials in the upper elementary grades include activities for children to practice reading maps and interpreting map symbols. Children learn to read the keys as they carry out assignments to find the state capital, a county seat, campsites, airports, and/or state forests. They use the scale to estimate distance (e.g., Albany to Buffalo) and the compass rose to give the direction. Children need to develop conventional map reading skills. These skills do not, however, prepare a child to construct a map.

Children make a variety of decisions as they make a map. What are the criteria for making these decisions? With specific reference to symbols and keys, how do children decide about symbols and keys in their own maps?

Initially most children do not think of using symbols. Maps of bedrooms tend to be maps of several pieces of furniture, which are typically identified by drawing and/or labeling. When Felice introduced the notion of a key, some of her children embarked on a somewhat arbitrary effort to incorporate keys and symbols in their bedroom maps. Natalie's work (Figure 4-20) illustrates this. The key and use of symbols give no improvement over the initial drawing and labeling. On the other hand, when faced with the task of mapping the route from home to school, children began using symbols to reduce the magnitude of the task of representing all the things they pass.

Beginning Ideas of Scale

Notions of scaling come up in different ways. In Felice's class, children saw maps of a subway system and of the United States side-by-side. They were similar in size. The kids wondered how the maps could be the same size when the sizes of the real things were so different. Seeing these two maps that used vastly different scales implicitly raised the question of scale. Felice understood her children's problem as one that they could answer when they understood scaling.

Sandra Jenoure's fifth-grade class was attempting to map the cafeteria as a first step in redesigning the placement of the waste receptacles. Jose asked: "How can we get the whole cafeteria on this piece of paper?" Jose's problem too was one of understanding scale and, in his case, being able to apply scale to the mapping of a large room. How do children begin to understand scale?

Prerequisite to an understanding of scale is that children have a feeling for proportion. This is seen when children recognize that aspects of a map are out of proportion. Karen Nelson, a teacher at P.S. 174 in the Bronx, had her fourth-graders draw floor plans of the classroom. Sasha drew desks that filled the whole space so there was no room for aisles or space at the front or back of the room. "It looks like there's no room to move, but there really is." Juan, with his tiny drawings of desks, ended up with the opposite result: "We don't have this much empty space." Such statements show children as they recognize a lack of proportion or a lack of correspondence between the map space and the real space. They begin to appreciate things drawn to scale.

Locate Your Place with Coordinates and Grids

Michael Gatton, a middle school science teacher, introduced the use of coordinates in mapping by having his eighth graders locate their desk with reference to "landmarks" on the walls.

Students imagined straight lines coming out of the walls, one set connecting the front and back walls, another set connecting both side walls. The imagined lines produce a grid of invisible intersecting perpendicular lines. A location on the grid is identified by two references: the point on the front wall from which an imagined line passes through one's desk, and the point on the side wall from which another imagined line, perpendicular to the wall, passes through the desk. The intersection of the two imagined lines locates a particular student's desk.

4-32: **William's use of landmarks for locating his desk**

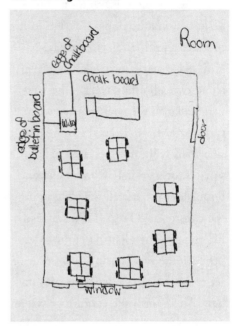

Figure 4-32 shows how William located his desk. He imagined a line through his desk to the front of the room. It hit the edge of the chalkboard. A similar line to the wall at his left hit the edge of the bulletin board. These two "landmarks" are the coordinates of his desk. The intersection of the lines from each of these points marks the location of William's desk.

William used landmarks (recognizable points along the wall) to locate his desk. Landmarks along the edge do not produce a grid. To begin to make a grid, place marks at regular intervals along two adjoining walls. Lines perpendicular to the wall are drawn from each mark. Lines from the front and side walls will form a pattern of squares, or a grid. The lines between floor tiles form a ready-made grid in the classroom. The grid is made ready for mapping by identifying the spaces between the marks using a consecutive set of symbols, usually letters or numbers. These form the coordinate system of the map or room. (See Figure 4-33.)

In commercial maps, a combination of letters and numbers identifies the coordinates. Typically letters of the alphabet are placed along the vertical side of the grid and numbers along the horizontal side. To find the location of a street in the map of our city, we find the street name in the index and get

the coordinates of its location, say B-3. On the map we read across from the letter B and down from the number 3 to the place where the two coordinates intersect. That quadrant is where we look for the street. We can use coordinates when making a map as well as when using it. If we number the tiles across the front of the room and place letters on the tiles down the side of the room, then the floor tiles will provide the same sort of grid for the class room as we find on a street map.

Games for Grids and Coordinates

Teachers use mapping games to develop a range of mapping skills. Two of the games developed by the Elementary Science Study project are especially good for developing the skills of using grids and coordinates: "Checkers" and "Tic-Tac-Toe." Angel Gonzalez calls these "Blind Checkers" and "Blind Tic-Tac-Toe" because the players' moves are hidden from one another.

The games are played by setting up two identical game boards separated by a screen that hides each board from the opposing player. To play, a player makes a move, then describes it to his opponent so that she can replicate the move on her board. She then makes her responding move, communicates it to her opponent, and he replicates

it on his board. The game continues until there is a winner, or until there is such confusion that the game is stopped for the players to remove the screen and compare the two boards. The boards should be identical. Differences are signs of miscommunication.

"Tic-Tac-Toe," using only a three-by-three grid, is by far the easiest. Children quickly figure out how to communicate these simple positions. Players may describe their moves in terms of rows and columns, but they can play successfully using terms such as "top-left," "top-middle," or "middle-right." This game is good preparation for "Blind Checkers."

"Blind Checkers," played on an eight-by-eight grid, is by far the greater challenge. To describe a move, the player must describe the beginning and ending position of the piece that is moved. "Right," "middle," and "left" are no longer adequate to describe the column and "top," "middle," and "bottom" no longer describe the row. The need to identify a particular quadrant among the 64 provides the pressure for children to develop the ability to see the board as a grid and to impose some sort of coordinates upon the grid. There are usually a number of aborted games before children work out a way to communicate a particular position.

4-33: Coordinate system

	1	2	3	4	5
A					
B					
C					
D					
E					

First Steps to Scale

Perhaps the simplest way for children to make a scale drawing of the classroom is to begin with floor tiles (where possible) as the unit for mapping. Let one floor tile be one square on the graph paper. Children count the number of tiles across the room, and its length in tiles. From this they outline the room on graph paper. They count the number of tiles from the corner of the room to the door and mark off a similar number of squares on the graph paper. They count the number of tiles across the door opening, then the number to the teacher's desk, again marking the corresponding squares on the graph paper. They map furniture in the same way. They see which tiles are covered by the teacher's desk. The corresponding squares on the graph paper are outlined and labeled "Teacher's Desk." This process of making one-to-one correspondences between tiles in the room and squares in the graph paper continues until the room is mapped. The resulting map is a scale map, drawn to the scale of one tile to one square.

When children construct a one-tile-to-one-square map, they do not need to understand ratio and proportion to construct it. Rather, children begin to develop the notion of ratio and proportion through constructing the map. By keeping a constant relationship between floor tiles and squares, a map is drawn in which tables and desks have the same positions on the map as they do in the room.

Angel Gonzalez provided his fifth-graders with a map of the perimeter of the room and its fixed furniture. He drew this "master map" on graph paper where four squares equal 1 inch, using a scale of one square to one floor tile. The task for each group of children was to locate their desks in the room, draw them, and then locate and draw the desks of the other groups. Angel showed students how to locate a desk by counting the tiles from the point where the desk is situated to the front (or back) of the room, and then counting the tiles from the same point (where the desk is situated) to the side of the room. By demonstrating on a scaled up (1 inch = 1 floor tile) version of the "master map" of the room, Angel showed his students how to use the number of tiles they had counted to map the location of their desks.

The task Angel set for his children included not only locating their desks, but also drawing them to the same scale as the map. Just as kids measured the distance from desk to wall in tiles, so they measured the length and width of their desks in tiles. Thus, if the desks covered an area seven tiles in one direction and five in another, the drawings of their desks would cover a map space of seven squares by five squares.

Going Beyond "One Tile = One Square"

Mapping one tile to one square does not fully address the question of Jose: "How do we get the whole cafeteria on this sheet of paper?" That has to do with understanding scale and the need for it. Felice helped children see the need for scale when it became clear that the scale of one tile to one square that worked for a portion of the room (the rug) would not work for the whole room. The 1-inch square paper did not come in large enough sheets. How then could the room be represented on the sheets that were available? The idea of mapping a two-tile length as a one square length on the paper was the solution. As we see in her account, many children found the use of a 2:1 ratio very difficult. The point at which they really had trouble was when dealing with fewer than two tiles. This led to fractional parts of the graph paper square. Two-to-one ratios are much easier when the tiles come in groups of two. Note that they were using the 2:1 ratio to construct cut-outs of the area covered by their desks, not the whole classroom. They were to fit their 2:1 scaled desks into the 2 tiles to 1 square master map of the classroom constructed by Felice. Fifth-graders are at the beginning of being able to use scale in constructing maps of the simplest things.

Evaluating Mapping

Felice, Angel, and Michael assessed children's mapping skills and understanding in different ways. Many of the assessments were embedded in the everyday work of the class. Talking with children is an efficient way to learn how they think about things. Angel's initial brainstorming and discussion with the children elicited baseline data on what they knew and what they wanted to know about mapping. At a later point, when he gave them a chance to express their understandings of north, he harvested a rich mixture of misunderstanding that he used to guide his planning.

Children's products, in this case maps, are the way we see their thinking in action. Talk may reveal an acquaintance with terms such as a map key or compass rose. Their maps show us how they make use of a key, or indeed if they see any use for one. When we see a compass rose drawn on a map with no concern for the direction of north in the area mapped, we know there are connections we have to help children make about the function of a compass rose. Children's first maps of their rooms, and their talk about the maps, gave Felice her initial cues as to what to emphasize.

When a student interprets another's map, and when he attempts to use another's map, the map user, the mapmaker, and the teacher can assess the map. Such assessment is seen in Felice's class as children try to make sense of each other's maps from home to school: Can they figure out the route actually taken? How easy or difficult is it to read the map? How could the map be improved? Felice also puts maps of the classroom to actual use. Could one student follow the route mapped by another?

Michael's students had mapped diffusion during the semester. He included an aspect of mapping in his end-of-term examination. He presented them with a map of the classroom and a spilled bottle of perfume in the corner, a location with which they had no direct experience. The task was to draw a series of five gradient lines showing how the odor would spread under ideal conditions of no air currents. They then shaded the map from region of strongest concentration to weakest. Students found this sort of problem-solving to be considerably more difficult than the more common short answer test item.

Chapter 5
RESOURCES
Help for Teachers

Making Connections with Literature

Using literature as a supplement and enhancement for instruction is good teaching practice because:

- Children learn from everything they experience.
- Children learn more effectively when instruction is associated with positive emotions, such as those evoked by a good book.
- Literacy is key to children's success as learners.
- There are many different learning styles.

We encourage you to incorporate books of all kinds into your work with *Mapping*. We've included an annotated list of quality books of all kinds on the following pages. They include storybooks in which main characters map out their travels, books with maps of historical events and places, and "how-to" books on map-making and mapping terms.

But don't stop with these. You know your students and how they learn better than anyone else. When you see a book that might further your instructional goals, interest or challenge a particular student, or evoke feelings that make learning more fun, add it to the books that are available to your students.

Amelia Hits the Road, by Marissa Moss. Pleasant Company: Middleton, Wisconsin, 1999. (Recommended grades: 3-6)
Ten-year-old Amelia keeps a journal of the summer car trip she takes with her family. This third volume of Amelia's handwritten notebooks, filled with graphics, proves that vacation and travel journal-writing can not only have a purpose, but can also be fun.

Amelia's Road, by Linda Jacobs Altman. Lee & Low Books, Inc.: New York, 1995. (Recommended grades: 1-5)
Amelia hates all roads and all maps until she creates a map of her own. The daughter of migrant farm workers, she is weary of wandering and dreams of a home of her own.

Anno's Journey, by Mitsumasa Anno. The Putnam Publishing Group: New York, 1997. (Recommended Grades: K-3)
With pictures that need no words, Anno relates the story of his journey through Northern Europe and his impressions of the land and the people at work and play.

Araminta's Paint Box, by Karen Ackerman. MacMillan Publishing: New York, 1998. (Recommended grades: 1-5)
Araminta and her paint box are each going to make it to the West Coast, but by divergent routes, as shown on the map with its map key.

Around the World in a Hundred Years: From Henry the Navigator to Magellan, by Jean Fritz. Putnam Publishing Group: New York, 1998. (Recommended grades: 3-6)
The chapters in this book are arranged in chronological succession, showing us the dangers, real and imaginary, that were faced by early explorers when they ventured into the unknown.

As the Crow Flies: A First Book of Maps, by Gale Hartman. Bradbury Press: New York, 1991. (Recommended grades: K-3)
This is a first book on the purpose and process of mapping. It explores the journeys of an eagle, a rabbit, a crow, a police horse, and a gull, following each with a map of the described path.

The Berenstain Bears and the Big Road Race, by Stan Berenstain and Jan Berenstain. Random House: New York, 1987. (Recommended grades: K-3)
"Over, under, around and through went Orange, Yellow, Green and Blue," but Brother Bear in his little red car slowly but surely wins out.

The Book of Where, or, How to Be Naturally Geographic, by Neill Bell. Little, Brown & Company: Boston, 1982. (Recommended grades: 3-6)
A geography book designed to teach children direction and map reading through activities that outline the basic concepts of geography; scale, maps, the globe, continental plates, and oceans. You will find its greatest use as an independent study guide to supplement classroom instruction.

The Case of the Backyard Treasure, by Joanne Rocklin. Scholastic Inc.: New York, 1998. (Recommended grades: 2-5)

Liz the Whiz and her younger brother use codes, a chart, and a map of the backyard that matches a clock face to solve Zack's mystery.

City: A Story of Roman Planning and Construction, by David Macaulay. Houghton Mifflin Co.: Boston, 1983. (Recommended grades: 4-6 and teacher resource)

This book teaches how Roman cities were built in 25 B.C. The text, and black and white illustrations show how the Romans planned, mapped out, and constructed their cities.

Cool Geography: Miles of Maps, Wild Adventures, Fun Activities, Facts from Around the World and More! by Jane Glicksman. Putnam Publishing: New York, 1998. (Recommended grades: 4-6)

Cool Geography goes around the world, describing its maps, hemispheres, continents, countries, and people. Each page is packed full of maps, early explorer information, brain busters and very cool activities that involve students with creating their own maps to scale.

Evan's Corner, by Elizabeth Starr Hill. Penguin Putnam Books: New York, 1992. (Recommended grades: PreK-3)

Evan's family lives in a crowded apartment too small for privacy, but Evan's mother lets him choose his own special corner. Evan maps out the room, picks a corner by the window, and makes the space his own.

Exploring the Night Sky, by Terence Dickenson. Firefly Books: Buffalo, 1987. (Recommended grades: 4-6+)

An excellent introduction to astronomy for the beginner, targeted for young adults but can be enjoyed by all ages. There are sky maps of constellations and planets, and introductions to key vocabulary and concepts. Vivid illustrations throughout are included on different angles of sky mapping.

Follow the Drinking Gourd, by Jeanette Winter. Alfred A. Knopf: New York, 1992. (Recommended grades: PreK-6)

What sounded like a simple folk song sung by slaves was actually a set of directions to help slaves follow the Underground Railroad and escape to freedom. They would find the Underground Railroad heading north, by following the "drinking gourd" of the Big Dipper.

Geography Wizardry, by Margaret Elizabeth Kenda. Barron's Educational Series: Hauppauge, NY, 1997. (Recommended grades: 3-6+)

Introduces the world of maps and mapmaking, orientation, and scale. Contains over 150 fun projects, maps, and experiments for junior explorers.

Grasshopper on the Road, by Arnold Lobel. HarperCollins: New York, 1986. (Recommended grades: K-3)

In this "I Can Read Book Series: Level 2" book, Grasshopper wanted to go on a journey. In following the road wherever it goes, he meets some unusual characters.

Henry and the Paper Route, by Beverly Cleary. William Morrow & Co.: New York, 1990. (Recommended grades: 3-6)

Henry wants to have a paper route and he's sure he can prove to the route manager that he is responsible to handle the job. Henry's plans go awry, and he needs to get help from an unlikely source in order to make his paper route a success.

How to Make an Apple Pie and See the World, by Marjorie Priceman. Random House: New York, 1996. (Recommended grades: PreK-3)

When an energetic little baker discovers that the market is closed, she travels the world via various modes of transportation to find the freshest ingredients for her apple pie.

I Read Signs, by Tana Hoban. Morrow, William & Co.: New York,1987. (Recommended grades: PreK-2)

The author uses photographs to introduce signs and symbols frequently seen along the street.

I Read Symbols, by Tana Hoban. Greenwillow Books: New York, 1996. (Recommended grades: PreK-2)

This book introduces signs and symbols that are frequently seen along the highway.

Kids Learn America!: Bring Geography to Life with People, Places and History, by Patricia Gordon and Reed C. Snow. Williamson Publishing: Charlotte, VT, 1999. (Recommended grades: 1-6)

The reader is taken on an exciting journey across America and celebrates the achievers and the achievements that shaped this nation—from long ago right up to the present. The geography, history, and culture of the states and territories of the United States are surveyed using maps, charts, and illustrations.

The Magic School Bus Inside the Human Body, by Joanna Cole and Bruce Degen. Scholastic, Inc.: New York, 1990. (Recommended grades: 2-6)

A special field trip on the magic school bus allows Ms. Frizzle's class to get a first-hand look at major parts of the body and how they work.

Mapping the World, by Sylvia A. Johnson. Simon & Schuster: New York, 1999. (Recommended grades: 3-6)

In a clear and informative progression, this history of mapmaking shows how maps both reflect and change peoples' view of the world.

Maps: Getting from Here to There, by Harvey Weiss. Houghton Mifflin Company: Boston, 1995 (Recommended grades: 3-6)

This book describes the many different kinds of maps and explains the methods that mapmakers use to convey information and simple explanations of scale, latitude, longitude and altitude.

Maps & Globes, by Jack Knowlton. HarperCollins Children's Books: New York, 1986. (Recommended grades: 1-6)

This book presents a brief history of mapmaking, its place in exploration, the use of scale, and the advantages of globes over flat maps.

Maps and Globes, by David Lambert. The Bookwright Press: New York, 1987. (Recommended grades: 3-6)

This book describes maps and globes of all kinds: how they are made, what they are used for, and how to understand them.

Maps and Mapping, by Barbara Taylor. Kingfisher Books: New York, 1993. (Recommended grades: K-6)

The information in this introduction to maps and mapmaking covers the elements found on maps, including scales, contour lines, latitude, and the use of colors and symbols.

Maps and Symbols, by Angela Royston. Raintree Steck-Vaughn: New York, 1998. (Recommended grades: 2-5)

This is an introduction to maps: what they represent, how they are constructed, and how to read them.

Me and My Place in Space, by Joan Sweeney. Crown Publishers: New York, 1999. (Recommended grades: K-6)

With earth as a starting point, a young astronaut describes how the earth, sun, and planets are part of our solar system, answering simple questions. A glossary in back helps reinforce new words and concepts.

Me on the Map, by Joan Sweeney. Crown Publishing: New York, 1998. (Recommended grades: K-3)

A child introduces the world of cartography. Using the premise that simple drawings can be maps, the book begins with crayon drawings of the floor plans of the girl's room and house.

My Place, by Nadia Wheatley. Kane/Miller Book Publishers: New York, 1994. (Recommended grades: 3-6)

A glimpse into life on the same piece of Australian land as it changes from rural to urban over a 200-year period from the viewpoints of children who live there. Each child describes what life is like, with intricately drawn maps labeled to help spot the changes that have taken place

My Place in Space, by Robin and Sally Hirst. Orchard Book: New York, 1992. (Recommended grades: K-3)

A rude bus driver asks Henry and his sister Rosie if they know where they live. Henry responds with detailed information: street, town, country, hemisphere, planet, solar system, solar neighborhood, Milky Way Galaxy, the universe. With each response, he gives a brief description of each part of the address, mapping it in the sky.

The Mystery of the Pirate's Map, by Gertrude Chandler Warner. Albert Whitman & Co.: Morton Grove, IL, 1999. (Recommended grades: 2-6)

While at a seaside resort visiting a friend of Grandfather's, the Boxcar Children find a long lost piece of a map to a legendary pirate treasure, a discovery that brings unwanted attention from fortune hunters.

Nine O'Clock Lullaby, by Marilyn Singer. HarperCollins: New York, 1993. (Recommended grades: K-3)

This book presents the world as a global village, beginning with a bedtime scene in Brooklyn, and following time zones eastward through scenes at more than a dozen places around the globe.

North, South, East, and West, by Allan Fowler. Children's Press: Chicago, 1993. (Recommended grades: 1-3)

This "Rookie Read-About Science" book gives a simple explanation of the four main directions when mapping, and tells how to use the sun to determine direction.

Off the Map: The Journals of Lewis and Clark, by Meriwether Lewis. Walker and Company: New York, 1998. (Recommended grades: 3-6)

A selection of entries and excerpts from the journals of Lewis and Clark, describes their historic expedition.

Oh, the Places You'll Go! by Dr. Seuss. Random House: New York, 1990. (Recommended grades: K-6 & Adults)

In this joyous ode to life and success, the author's message is that "Life may be a great balancing act, but through it all there's fun to be done."

On Board the Titanic, by Shelly Tanaka. Hyperion: New York, 1996. (Recommended grades: 5+)

The story of the Titanic is told through the eyes of two young survivors, with full color illustrations and detailed diagrams of ship's interior and room designs.

The Pirate's Handbook: How to Become a Rogue of the High Seas, by Margarette Lincoln. Dutton: New York, 1995. (Recommended grades: 2-6)

An entertaining guidebook that offers a glimpse into pirate legends and history. Activities include instructions for creating treasure maps and pirate flags.

Pirates: Robbers of the High Seas, by Gail Gibbon. Little, Brown & Company: Boston, 1999. (Recommended grades: K-3)

This book describes the lives of pirates, the ships they sailed, the maps they drew, and the types of treasure they stole.

Puzzle Maps U.S.A., by Nancy L. Clouse. Henry Holt & Company: New York, 1994. (Recommended grades: 2-6)

The book provides a basic introduction to map skills, covering the concepts of shape and proportion. It presents puzzle activities that utilize the different shapes of the states.

Rome Antics, by David Macaulay. Houghton Mifflin Company: Boston, 1996. (Recommended grades: 4-6)

A pigeon carrying an important message takes the reader on a unique tour through Rome. Scale and orientation are seen from a different time and a different point of view.

Squirrel's Treasure Hunt, by Annie Cobb. Silver Burdett Press: Englewood Cliffs, 1991. (Recommended grades: K-3)

Squirrel and Raccoon get lost on a treasure hunt because they can't follow directions. A bird helps them use their sense of direction and learn the four directions.

Sweet Clara and the Freedom Quilt, by Deborah Hopkinson. Alfred A Knopf: New York, 1995. (Recommended grades: K-6)

Based on a true, little known chapter in African-American history, this is the story of Clara, a young slave, who works as a seamstress and dreams of freedom. When she hears two slaves wishing for a map to the Underground Railroad, she begins to save scraps of colored cloth which she makes into a "freedom quilt," a patchwork map of an escape route that no Master will ever suspect.

The True Adventure of Daniel Hall, by Diane Stanley. Penguin Putnam Books: New York, 1999. (Recommended grades: K-4)

Using a 1861 autobiographical work by Hall called "Arctic Rovings," this book provides readers with a brief look at the exciting true adventure of a boy who left home at 14 to go on a whaling voyage. Atop each text page, a medallion features a map or an image from Daniel's adventure.

Walking the Road to Freedom: A Story About Sojourner Truth, by Jeri Ferris. Carolrhoda Books, Inc.: Minneapolis, 1991. (Recommended grades: 3-6)

This book includes a map of the travels of Sojourner Truth as she spoke out against slavery and campaigned for women's rights took her to more than 20 states.

Where Do I Live? by Neil Chesanow. Barron's Educational Series: Hauppauge, NY, 1995. (Recommended grades: K-5)

Young children learn in a concentric fashion where they live, as the book takes them from their bedroom, to their houses, then to the streets, neighborhoods etc., progressing all the way to the universe.

Where's Waldo?: The Fantastic Journey, by Martin Handford, Candlewick Press: Cambridge, MA, 1997. (Recommended grades: K-6)

Waldo embarks on fantastic journeys into lands full of Gobbling Gluttons, the Battling Monks, the Deep-sea Divers, the Underground Hunters, and the Land of Waldo in search of a special scroll.

Which Way to the Revolution: A Book About Maps, by Bob Barner. Holiday House, Inc.: New York, 1998. (Recommended grades: K-4)

This introduction to maps using familiar historical events adds a fantastic element to Paul Revere's ride when a group of friendly mice help him on his mission. Appended material includes brief notes on constructing maps and a summary of "The Ride."

The Wizard's Map, by Jane Yolen. Harcourt Brace & Co.: San Diego, 1999. (Recommended grades: 3-6)

Three children visiting relatives in Scotland, find a mysterious antique map that calls forth Michael Scott, a feared 700-year-old diabolical wizard. The Wizard's Map explores loyalty, love, and courage in the Harry Potter tradition.

Assessment

Nearly everyone agrees about the importance of assessment, but what exactly is it, and why is it so significant in education? In a very broad sense, education is like a very large design problem and assessment is the method of evaluating the design. However, education has many objectives, not just one, so assessment also includes a complex process of deciding what to assess and how. Another major complication is that many different kinds of people have a stake in the outcome of the educational process. Parents want to know how much their children are learning and how they can best help them. Politicians worry about the backlash from voters if the educational system appears to be "failing," however that term is defined. Administrators fear that they will be held accountable for low test scores in their schools.

Teachers, who have the most sustained and direct involvement of any adults in the educational process, are constantly looking for ways of knowing how well and how much their students are learning. This data can come from both formal and informal assessment methods, and may be either qualitative or quantitative. At the same time, teachers are often held accountable to conflicting requirements that are difficult or impossible to meet. For example, the goal of providing a supportive and welcoming learning environment may be in conflict with the regimentation imposed by administrative requirements. Another common concern of teachers is that high-stakes testing will require them to "teach to the test" rather than to support student learning.

Regardless of demands from outside the classroom, a teacher's primary responsibility is to engage students in exploring and understanding the subject matter. Assessment includes any method of finding out how much of this exploring and understanding actually happens. Information gained through assessment is the only factual basis for knowing what students are learning, how to motivate learning more effectively, how and whether to redesign the curriculum, how to tailor it to the needs of individual students, and how and when to involve parents in the process. Assessment is far too extensive and important to be narrowly defined by standardized test results or to be determined by people outside the classroom.

Here are some basic conclusions that follow from this view of assessment:

- Assessment should be based on clear educational goals.
- Many different kinds of information should be collected as part of assessment. Some of the most important assessment data is totally unexpected.
- Assessment should not be divorced from curriculum; every learning activity should also provide information for assessment.
- Whenever possible, students should become involved in assessing their own learning—for example, by evaluating their own designs or predictions.
- Assessment should examine not only what students have learned, but also the opportunities provided by the curriculum and the learning environment.

We will illustrate each of these points using examples from the teacher stories in Chapter 4.

Educational Goals

In order to assess the learning outcomes of an activity, it is necessary to know what the educational goals were. However, the purpose of a curriculum unit may not be so clear-cut. Any worthwhile educational activity probably has more than one goal. Also, a teacher's goals may (and often do) change as the activity progresses, or there may be unintended outcomes that are far more significant than the original goals. In thinking about assessment, it is important to regard educational goals in a broad flexible way.

Felice Piggott's mapping curriculum progressed from informal maps of bedrooms to a scale map of the classroom. Her goals included children's understanding and use of perspective, orientation, and scale. She planned a number of activities through which she could continually assess children's mastery of these concepts/skills. Like most of us, she wanted her kids to have a positive experience, to get involved in and excited about mapping. The problem with affective and attitudinal goals is one of measurement. Teachers know when things are going well, but what is there to show for evidence?

Part of the attraction of teaching is that much of what happens in the classroom is unpredictable, and some of the surprises are pleasant or even thrilling! Consequently, it is impossible to decide in advance what all of the methods of assessment will be. Often, serendipity provides ways of assessing students' learning that nobody could have anticipated. After Felice's class completed the classroom mapping project, they wanted to continue with an even larger project that would extend beyond their classroom. When children want to continue and expand upon prior work, it is an evaluation of the extent to which that work is internalized and valued.

Rigid adherence to an initial set of goals assumes that the educational process is entirely predictable, which is

not the case. Every teacher has both short- and long-term goals for her children's education, and it is difficult to know in advance when something will happen to advance the long-term goals unexpectedly. As one teacher put it during a discussion on assessment, "You can talk about goals all you want, but what I really care about is that they feel good about themselves and about what they are able to accomplish."

Information from a Variety of Sources

If educational goals are complex and multi-faceted, so are the means of assessing to what extent these goals are met. The narrowest view of assessment, most popular in political circles, confines it to standardized tests. A somewhat broader view expands assessment to include all kinds of paper-and-pencil instruments designed specifically for assessment, such as worksheets, homework assignments, tests, and quizzes.

Our view of assessment is broader still. In the course of an activity, nearly anything students do generates information that is valuable for assessment. When students talk about their ideas, they provide useful data about their understanding. In Minerva Rivera's class, children showed their diverse understanding of maps when

they brought in what they considered to be examples of maps from the daily newspaper. Their examples ranged from weather maps to TV listings to comic strips. Their understandings became clear in discussion:

- Shona: My group doesn't think a cartoon is a map. What does it have to do with directions?
- Julian: Maps don't have to show you where to go. It's exchanging dialog.
- Nicole: A map is not fiction. Cartoons are fiction.

When teachers use curricular activities as a window to children's thinking, they have a valid basis for planning subsequent activities.

Curriculum as a Major Source of Assesssment Data

In order to maximize the amount of information available, the curriculum itself must be seen as a rich source of assessment data. As children discuss their ideas and carry out projects, they reveal their strengths and weaknesses more clearly than they do through more formal assessment devices. Linda Crew began a mapping unit by displaying several maps, including one of her desk, and asking, "What kind of information do these maps give us?"

After a few student responses she writes:

**I wanted some feedback . . .
on the kinds of things we could get
from maps. So I started asking them
questions like:**

- **How many books are on
  may desk?**
- **Where is one object in relation
  to another?**
- **Is there a stapler on my desk?**

**They responded by using the map
without running to my desk. Based
on their answers it was clear to me
that they understood how to get
information from maps.**

Virtually any activity associated with
a curriculum unit can provide insights to
children's command of knowledge and
skills. Brainstorming sessions, scavenger
hunts, design activities, presentations to
the class, journals, and discussions within
a work group are all potential sources
of assessment information.

Students Assess
Their Own
Learning

Should the audience for assessment
data include students themselves?
Obviously, students need to know
how well they are doing, so they can
gauge their own efforts and develop
realistic goals for their own learning.
However, traditional assessment
is usually presented to students in an

adversarial manner, in the form of test
grades and report cards that frequently
undermine rather than enhance their
motivation for learning. In traditional
forms of assessment, students are
always evaluated by adults rather than
by themselves, and the outcomes of
assessment often have high stakes. Both
of these factors contribute to the
view of assessment as an antagonistic
process. How can students gain access
to candid data about their own
learning and performance, without
interpreting it as somehow the product
of bad intentions?

A way out of this dilemma is
suggested by some of the activities in
Chapter 4. Mapping activities often
provide occasions for self-assessment,
where students evaluate their own work
against an objective standard, rather
than one arbitrarily set by adults. In
Felice Piggott's room, children's maps
were regularly posted around the room
and analyzed by other children. After
posting the maps of the route from
home to school, one child would
study a classmate's map and then give a
narrative of how the map-maker got
from home to school. The map-maker
confirmed or rejected the narrative.
When the narrative was wrong, it
became the basis for analyzing what in
the map had been misunderstood.

Assessing the
Learning
Environment

Like anybody else who designs or plans
anything, most teachers engage in
informal assessment of their work
They ask themselves, "Is it working?"
This question is really one of self-
assessment: "What is the quality of the
learning opportunities I have provided
for my students?"

Some of this self-assessment by
teachers is based on student learning
outcomes, of the many kinds described
above. At the same time, teachers also
assess learning opportunities on the
basis of their own perceptions and
experiences. Several examples of these
self-assessments appear in the teachers'
stories in Chapter 4.

Felice was constantly reflecting
on the curricular decisions she had
made. She writes about the activity
of mapping a route in the classroom:

**Generally the kids enjoy the
mapping exercises and appear to
look forward to them, but for
many of them it's a really challenging
task. More time was needed for
sharing by the whole group. Sharing
occurred with the small groups working together, but whole class sharing
is also needed. I think we should
have walked through a few more
"dry runs" before we committed to
paper. Some kids were very confused
about direction and perspective.**

The Institutional Context

Every school is different. Each one offers both resources that can be helpful in implementing a new curriculum, and barriers that can make it difficult. It is useful to analyze both carefully, with an eye to mobilizing and extending the resources and overcoming the barriers. In this section, we will look at how some teachers have gained crucial support from school staff, parents, other teachers, and administrators as they developed new programs in science and technology.

The Custodian

The custodian is a key person in the success of any new program, particularly one such as Mapping, which may take students outside of the classroom and into the rest of the building. The custodian is probably more familiar with the physical layout of the building than anyone else. He or she also has the best access to discarded materials, such as cardboard, waste paper, or wood, that can be very useful. A cooperative custodian can also offer suggestions about additional storage space, and can insure that projects in process will not be thrown out.

The custodian's involvement can also lead to exciting surprises, as the following story illustrates. A second-grade teacher and her class were studying the water supply system of a school in the South Bronx, New York City. They began with the water fountain just outside their classroom. The children were convinced that the water for the fountain was stored in the wall just behind it. Then somebody noticed that there were pipes leading to the fountain. They followed the pipes along the ceiling and realized that they came from someplace else in the building. At this point they went to another floor and noticed a similar pattern of pipes. Eventually, their investigation led them to the basement. There they met the custodian, who gave them copies of the blueprints (maps) of the building, and showed them how the water came into the building. The following day, he gave them an opportunity to turn on the boiler, so they could see how the hot water was heated! The outcome of this investigation was a working 3D model of the building's water supply, in which the pipes were represented by straws and the reservoir by a basin held above the highest floor.

Parents

Parents can also be critical to the success of a curriculum project. A number of teachers have involved parents in investigations of the community around the school. One ESL teacher in East Harlem, New York City, whose students were recent immigrants from various parts of Latin America, engaged her students in a study of the casitas in the community. A *casita* (literally, "little house") is a small building constructed by community residents on a vacant lot, which may serve as a clubhouse or a religious shrine, or which may be used to house livestock. Several parents who were very familiar with the community accompanied the class on their field visits and facilitated their discussions with the users of the casitas.

How does a teacher get parents involved in the first place? Some teachers have organized parent/child workshops, after school or on Saturdays, as a way to inform parents of what their children are doing and to solicit their support. One strategy that has worked is to have a parent/child workshop a few weeks after children have begun a project.

In the workshop, parents and their children are encouraged to pursue a hands-on project that is similar to what the children have already been doing in school. Because the children have already started the project, they will often take the lead in explaining the material and offer their parents advice on how to proceed. At the same time, parents will provide their own experiences and expertise, and some may become excited enough to volunteer additional support. Parent volunteers can provide the additional adult presence needed for taking the class outside the building.

Other Teachers

Just as children often require peer interaction to pursue a project, so peer support can be essential for teachers too. Another teacher can be a springboard for ideas, a source of advice on overcoming difficulties, and a friend to turn to when everything seems to go wrong. There are many models for teacher/teacher collaboration, each of which can work in some circumstances. Ultimately, the collaborators have to figure out for themselves what works best for them. Here are some examples of ways in which teachers in the same school have worked together:

An experienced teacher gave workshops in the school, in which she engaged other teachers in some of the same activities she had been doing in her classroom. Several of the other teachers became interested and sought advice on pursuing these activities in their own classrooms.

An experienced special education teacher mentored a less experienced special ed teacher, offering her assistance in some of the same projects she had done in her own classroom.

A science cluster teacher met with a classroom group during a "prep" period twice a week. She enlisted the students' classroom teacher in pursuing some of the same projects as part of their regular classroom work.

A fifth grade teacher and a kindergarten teacher decided to work together. After the fifth-graders had pursued some of their own investigations, several of them became the facilitators in helping the kindergarten children do similar studies. The work involved cataloging and mapping what they found in nearby empty lots. Besides a collaboration among teachers, this project was also a collaboration between older and younger children.

Collaboration among teachers may be actively discouraged by the culture of the school. Even in the best circumstances, collaborations can be difficult to sustain. Just as every school is different, so is every classroom. Ideas and strategies that work in one classroom may or may not be directly transferable to another, and it is important to remain sensitive to differences in chemistry and culture from one room to the next. The most important ingredient in collaboration among teachers is the commitment to work and learn together, regardless of the outcome of any particular project or idea.

School Administration

A major component of a teacher's setting is the culture of the school administration. A principal, assistant principal, or other supervisor can make or break an innovative curriculum project. Some teachers are fortunate enough to find themselves in environments that nurture innovation; others are not so lucky. For better or worse, the tone set by the administration is a major factor that every teacher has to deal with. Even without initial support, however, there are a number of strategies for bringing a skeptical (or even a hostile) administrator on board.

One teacher, who was a participant in an in-service inquiry science program, had a roomful of upper-elementary students engaged in long-term science investigations, largely of their own design. She decided to encourage them to enter their projects in the school science fair. She immediately ran into the opposition of her principal, who insisted that all of the material on the display boards be "professionally done." The teacher knew that her students were invested in their projects, and perfectly capable of creating their own displays, but unable to type the material or produce fancy graphics. To make the displays for them would be to undermine all of their efforts and enthusiasm. So she presented the situation to her children, without any suggestion about what they ought to do about it.

The next time the principal visited their classroom, the students let him know that they wanted to enter the science fair, and they believed they could make display boards which would be perfectly readable. In any case, they would be around to explain anything the judges didn't understand. With the teacher standing by silently, the principal reluctantly gave in. At the fair, it became clear that these were the students who had the best grasp of their own projects, although there were others that had nicer-looking boards. Neither the children nor the teacher were surprised when they won first, second, and third prizes, and went on to the District fair! Equally important, the teacher felt that this was a turning point in her relationship with the principal. Afterwards, he interfered much less with her efforts at innovation.

It is far more effective to mobilize children, parents, other teachers, and staff than to confront an administrator directly. He or she will have a much harder time saying no to children, parents, or a group of teachers than to an individual. Also, successful programs speak for themselves. Outside authorities, such as science fair judges, funding sources, or important visitors, can make even the most reluctant principal sit up and take notice. Most important, innovation succeeds best when innovators lay the seeds quietly over time, and exploit opportunities to overcome resistance.

Resist the temptation to take on every adversary, every time. Focus instead on the resources that are available to you, and learn how to mobilize them effectively. Wait for opportunities to let your efforts speak for themselves.

Chapter 6

ABOUT STANDARDS

Overview

In Chapter 3, "Activities," we have listed standards references for each activity. This type of listing is now found in most curriculum materials, in order to demonstrate that the activities "meet standards." In a way, these standards references miss the point, because the national standards are not meant to be read in this way. Meeting standards is not really about checking off items from a list. Each of the major standards documents is a coherent, comprehensive call for systematic change in education.

This chapter shows how *Stuff That Works!* is consistent with national standards at a very fundamental level. We will look in detail at the following documents:

- *Standards for Technological Literacy: Content for the Study of Technology* (International Technology Education Association, 2000);
- *Benchmarks for Science Literacy* (American Association for the Advancement of Science, 1993);
- *National Science Education Standards* (National Research Council, 1996);
- *Principles and Standards for School Mathematics* (National Council of Teachers of Mathematics, 2000);

- *Standards for the English Language Arts* (National Council of Teachers of English & International Reading Association, 1996); and
- *Curriculum Standards for the Social Studies* (National Council for the Social Studies, 1994).

Most of these standards are now widely accepted as the basis for state and local curriculum frameworks. The first document on the list is included because it is the only national standard focused primarily on technology. The *New Standards Performance Standards* (National Center on Education and the Economy, 1997) is based almost entirely on the B*enchmarks, National Science Education Standards,* the original NCTM Math *Standards* (1989) and the *Standards for the English Language Arts.*

Although they deal with very different disciplines, these major national standards documents have many remarkable similarities:

- They are aimed at *all* students, not only those who are college-bound.
- Using terms like "literacy" and "informed citizen," they argue that education should prepare students to understand current issues and participate in contemporary society.

- They recommend that school knowledge be developed for its use in solving real problems rather than as material "needed" for passing a test. They strongly endorse curriculum projects that arise from students' own ideas, experiences, and interests.
- They focus on the "big ideas" of their disciplines as opposed to memorization of isolated facts or training in narrowly defined skills. In other words, fewer concepts should be dealt with in greater depth. As the *National Science Education Standards* express it, "Coverage of great amounts of trivial, unconnected information must be eliminated from the curriculum" (NRC, 1996, p. 213).
- The standards reject standardized tests as the sole or even the major form of assessment. Traditional exams measure only what is easy to measure rather than what is most important. "While many teachers wish to gauge their students' learning using performance-based assessment, they find that preparing students for machine-scored tests—which often focus on isolated skills rather than contextualized learning—diverts valuable

classroom time away from actual performance." (NCTE/IRA, 1996, p. 7) The standards promote authentic assessment measures, which require students to apply knowledge and reasoning "to situations similar to those they will encounter outside the classroom" (NRC, 1996, p. 78). Furthermore, assessment should become "a routine part of the ongoing classroom activity rather than an interruption" and it should consist of "a convergence of evidence from different sources" (NCTM, 2000, p. 23).

- They highlight the roles of quantitative thinking, as well as oral and written communication, in learning any subject, and they emphasize the interdisciplinary character of knowledge.
- They view learning as an active process requiring student engagement with the material and subject to frequent reflection and evaluation by both teacher and learner.
- They urge teachers to "display and demand respect for the diverse ideas, skills and experiences of all students," and to "enable students to have a significant voice in decisions about the content and context of their work." (NRC, 1996, p. 46)

The *Stuff That Works!* materials are based on these ideas and provide extensive guidance on how to implement them in the classroom. We begin our study of technology with students' own ideas and experiences, address problems that are of importance to them, develop "big ideas" through active engagement in analysis and design, and draw connections among the disciplines. While the standards are clear about the principles, they do not provide many practical classroom examples. *Stuff That Works!* fills this gap.

Where the Standards Came From

Historically speaking, the current tilt towards national curriculum standards is a dramatic departure from a long tradition of local control of education. How did national standards manage to become the order of the day? In the late 1970's, the country was in a serious recession, driven partly by economic competition from Europe and Japan. In 1983, the National Commission on Educational Excellence (NCEE) published an influential report, *A Nation at Risk,* which painted a depressing picture of low achievement among the country's students. The report warned of further economic consequences should these problems continue to be ignored, and advocated national curriculum standards for all students. Adding to these arguments were pressures from textbook publishers, who felt that national standards would make state and local adoption processes more predictable.

Around the same time, several of the major professional organizations decided to provide leadership in setting standards. The pioneering organizations were the National Council of Teachers of Mathematics (NCTM) and the American Association for the Advancement of Science (AAAS), whose efforts culminated in the publication of major documents in 1989. In the same year, the National Governors' Association and the Bush Administration both endorsed the concept of establishing national educational goals. The NCTM was deeply concerned about the issues raised by *A Nation at Risk* and was convinced that professional educators needed to take the initiative in setting a new educational agenda. Otherwise, the reform of curriculum would rest in the hands of textbook and test publishers, legislatures, and local districts.

Both the NCTM and the AAAS standards projects began with a similar basic position about pedagogy. Influenced by research about what children actually know, they recognized the disturbing fact that "learning is not necessarily an outcome of teaching." (AAAS, 1989, p. 145) In contrast with traditional approaches to education, which emphasize memorization and drill, the new national standards promote strategies for active learning. A related theme of the early standards efforts was that the schools should teach fewer topics in order that "students end up with richer insights and deeper understandings than they could hope to gain from a superficial exposure to more topics…" (p. 20). Meeting standards requires a major investment of time and resources. Some of the necessary ingredients include new curriculum ideas and materials, professional development opportunities, new assessment methods, and smaller class sizes. *The National Science Education Standards* are the most explicit in identifying the conditions necessary – at the classroom, school, district, and larger political levels—for standards to be meaningful. The authors state, "Students could not achieve standards in most of today's schools." (NRC, 1996, p. 13) More money might not even be the hardest part. Standards-based reforms also require understanding and commitment from everyone connected with the educational system, starting at the top.

The history of standards may contain clues about their future. Standards imply neither textbook-based instruction nor standardized tests. Standards arose because traditional text- and test-based education had failed to result in the learning of basic concepts by the vast majority of students. Ironically, there are many textbook and test purveyors who market their products under the slogan "standards-based." Standards could easily become discredited if those who claim their imprimatur ignore their basic message.

What the Standards Actually Mean

Standards are commonly read as lists of goals to be achieved through an activity or a curriculum. This approach is reflected in the lists of standards references and cross-references that appear in most curriculum materials, as evidence that an activity or curriculum "meets standards."

Presenting lists of outcomes reflects a narrow reading of standards, which can be very misleading. These lists suggest that "meeting standards" is simply a matter of getting students to repeat something like the statements found in the standards documents, such as the one quoted above.

In fact, the standards are much richer and more complex than these lists imply. Many of the standards do not even specify the knowledge that students should acquire, but deal rather with ways of using that knowledge. Here is an example from *Benchmarks for Science Literacy:*

"By the end of fifth grade, students should be able to write instructions that students can follow in carrying out a procedure." (p. 296)

This standard talks about something students should be *able to do,* rather than what they should *know.* The newly released NCTM document, *Principles and Standards for School Mathematics* (2000), unlike the earlier one (NCTM, 1989), explicitly separates "Content Standards" from "Process

Standards." The Content Standards outline what students should learn, while the Process Standards cite ways of acquiring and expressing the content knowledge. The Process Standards include problem solving, communication, and representation. The *Benchmarks* example just cited above is another example of a process standard. Similarly, in the English Language Arts (ELA) document (NCTE/IRA, 1996), all twelve standards use verbs to express what students should *do,* as opposed to what they should *know.* Any reading of standards that focuses only on content knowledge is missing a central theme of all of the major documents.

There is also material in the standards that qualifies neither as content nor as process. Here is an example from the *Benchmarks* chapter called "Values and Attitudes":

"By the end of fifth grade, students should raise questions about the world around them and be willing to seek answers to some of them by making careful observations and trying things out." (p. 285)

This standard asks for more than a specific piece of knowledge, ability, or skill. It calls for a way of looking at the world, a general conceptual framework that transcends the boundaries of disciplines. Similarly, the "Connections" standard in the new NCTM document underscores the need for students to …

"… Recognize and apply mathematics in contexts outside of mathematics." (NCTM, 2000, p. 65)

These are examples of broad curriculum principles that cut across the more specific content and process standards. These standards are not met by implementing a particular activity or by teaching one or another lesson. They require an imaginative search for opportunities based on a reshaping of goals for the entire curriculum.

In general, the standards documents are at least as much about general principles as about particular skills and knowledge bases. *The Standards for Technological Literacy,* the *Benchmarks,* and the *National Science Education Standards* each identifies some big ideas that recur frequently and provide explanatory power throughout science and technology. "Systems" and "modeling" are concepts that appear in all three documents. The presence of such unifying ideas suggests that the individual standards references should not be isolated from one another. They should rather be seen as parts of a whole, reflecting a few basic common themes.

*W*hat Use Are Standards?

Increasingly, teachers are being held accountable for "teaching to standards." These demands are added to such other burdens as paperwork, test schedules, classroom interruptions, inadequate space and budgets, arbitrary changes in class roster, etc.

In the view of many teachers, children and their education are routinely placed at the end of the priority list. Understandably, teachers may resent or even resist calls to "meet standards" or demonstrate that their curricula are "standards-bearing." It is not surprising that many teachers cynically view the standards movement as "another new thing that will eventually blow over."

The push to "meet standards" is often based on a misreading of standards as lists of topics to be "covered" or new tests to be administered. It is not hard to imagine where this misinterpretation might lead. If the proof of standards is that students will pass tests, and students fail them nevertheless, then the standards themselves may eventually be discarded. Paradoxically, the prediction that "this, too, shall pass" would then come true, not because the standards failed, but because they were never understood nor followed.

Standards are intended to demolish timeworn practices in education. Some of these practices place the teacher at the center of the classroom but reduce her or him to a cog in the machinery of the school and the district, with the primary responsibility of preparing students for tests. The standards documents recognize the need to regard teachers as professionals, students as active, independent learners, and tests as inadequate methods of assessing the full range of learning.

Within broad frameworks, the standards urge teachers to use their judgment in tailoring the curriculum to students' needs and interests. The NRC Science Standards, for example,

call for "teachers [to be] empowered to make the decisions essential for effective learning." (1996, p. 2) Neither teachers nor administrators should interpret standards as mechanisms for tightening control over what teachers and students do. While they are very clear about the goals of education, the standards are less specific about how to meet them. Innovative curriculum efforts such as *Stuff That Works!* fit very well within the overall scheme of standards.

Teachers who have tried to implement *Stuff That Works!* activities in their classrooms have often come away with a positive feeling about them. The following comments are typical:

- *The strengths of this unit are the opportunity to group students, work on communication skills, problem solve … and plan real life tests. I have watched my students go from asking simple yes/no questions to thinking and planning careful, thoughtful active questions. The students began to see each other as people with answers… I was no longer the expert with all the answers.*

- *I must begin by telling you that I found this particular guide to be so much fun and the students demonstrated so much energy and interest in this area… I was able to engage them in the activities easily.. The activities were very educational and provided so much vital information that helped students connect what is being taught to them in math to real life situations, e.g., graphing behavior and using tallies to record information. For my [special education] students, I found this gave them self confidence…*

• *I read the entire guide from front to back... Although the main idea of the unit is not specifically a large focus of instruction in our fourth grade curriculum, I recognized the power behind the ideas and activities and knew that this unit would promote collaboration, problem solving and communication... Overall, I think my students loved this unit and felt enormously successful after we finished...*

• *My most important goal for students is that they feel good about them-selves and realize what they can do. I liked these activities, because they had these results.*

The standards are intended to promote just these sorts of outcomes. When a teacher has a "gut feeling" that something is working well, there is usually some basis to this feeling. As the NRC Science Standards state, "outstanding things happen in science classrooms today... because extraordi-nary teachers do what needs to be done *despite conventional practice* [emphasis added]." (1996, p. 12) Unfortunately, even an extraordinary teacher may not find support from traditional adminis-trators, who complain that the classroom is too noisy or messy, or that somebody's guidelines are not being followed. Under these circumstances, standards can be very useful. It is usually easy to see how valuable innovations fit into a national framework of education reform that is also endorsed by state- and district-level authorities. Standards can be used to justify and enhance innovative educational programs whose value is already self-evident to teachers and students.

What the Standards Really Say

In order to justify work as meeting standards, it is necessary to know what the standards really say. In the remainder of this chapter, we summarize each of the six major standards documents listed at the beginning of the chapter, and show how the *Stuff That Works!* ideas are consistent with these standards. We provide some historical background for each of the standards, and look at the overall intent and structure before relating them to the *Stuff That Works!* materials. These sections should be used only as they are needed. For example, if you would like to use some of the ideas from this Guide, and are also required to meet the *National Science Education Standards,* then that section could be useful to you in helping you justify your work.

Standards for Technological Literacy: Content for the Study of Technology

In April 2000, the International Technology Education Association (ITEA) unveiled the *Standards for Technological Literacy,* commonly known as the *Technology Content Standards,* after extensive reviews and revisions by the National Research Council (NRC) and the National Academy of

Engineering (NAE). In its general out-lines, the new standards are based on a previous position paper, *Technology for All Americans* (ITEA, 1996). The latter document defined the notion of "technological literacy" and promoted its development as the goal of technology education.

A technologically literate person is one who understands "what technology is, how it is created, and how it shapes society, and in turn is shaped by society." (ITEA, 2000, p. 9) According to the *Standards,* familiarity with these princi-ples is important not only for those who would pursue technical careers, but for all other students as well. They will need to know about technology in order to be thoughtful practitioners in most fields, such as medicine, journalism, business, agriculture, and education. On a more general level, technological liter-acy is a requirement for participation in society as an intelligent consumer and an informed citizen.

Given the importance of being technologically literate, it is ironic that technology barely exists as a school subject in the U.S., and is particularly hard to find at the elementary level. In a curriculum overwhelmingly focused on standardized tests, there seems to be little room for a new subject such as technology. To make matters worse, there is considerable confusion over what the term **technology** even means. Many in education still equate it with "computers." The *Standards* advocate for technology education based on a broad definition of "technology," which is "how humans modify the world around them to meet their needs and wants, or to solve practical problems." (p. 22)

The *Technology Content Standards* describe three aspects of developing technological literacy: learning *about* technology, learning to *do* technology, and technology as a theme for curriculum integration (pp. 4-9). To learn about technology, students need to develop knowledge not only about specific technologies (Standards 14–20), but also about the nature of technology in general (Standards 1–3), including its core concepts: **systems, resources, requirements, trade-offs, processes,** and **controls.** Resources include **materials, information,** and **energy,** while **modeling** and **design** are fundamental examples of processes (p. 33). Students learn to "do" technology by engaging in a variety of technological processes, such as **troubleshooting, research, invention, problem solving, use and maintenance, assessment** of technological impact, and, of course, **design** (Standards 8 – 13). Technology has obvious and natural connections with other areas of the curriculum, including not only math and science, but also language arts, social studies, and the visual arts.

The material in the *Stuff That Works!* guide *Mapping* offers numerous opportunities for learning the core concepts of technology. Whenever children construct a map they are dealing implicitly with the notion of system. The total area to be mapped comprises many systems, many groups of objects that interact with one another. In order to communicate the intended meanings, what things/systems must be included? What can be excluded?

Decisions to include or exclude representations on a map are at the heart of trade-offs. An example of the result of such trade-offs can be seen in Natalie's map of the route from home to school. Since Natalie takes the bus, she was faced with the problem of representing a considerable distance on the map, yet retaining details at either end of her trip. She had to decide what to omit and what to keep. The result was a map that those with the same frame of reference, namely bus-takers, could understand. However, her trade-offs resulted in a map that many could not understand, namely those who lacked her background experience.

Technology standards related to modeling are also addressed in mapping, although it is a special form of modeling. A first step in making a working model of a mechanism is to draw the mechanism in a way that maintains the proportions among its parts. This is essentially the process of mapping, of representing a three dimensional object in two dimensions. Maps are a special kind of model of reality: a model that reduces three dimensions to two dimensions. When a space is mapped, the reality is always far more complex than could ever be represented on a map. Thus the map is an abstraction of the reality, with the map-maker deciding what aspects of the space must be represented in the map.

According to the *Technology Content Standards,* design is "the core problem-solving process [of technology]. It is as fundamental to technology as inquiry is to science and reading is to language arts." (p. 91) The importance of design is underlined by the statement, a little further on, that "students in grades K-2 should learn that everyone can design solutions to a problem." (p. 93) Several pages later, the *Standards* suggest that young children's experiences in design should focus on "problems that relate to their individual lives, including their interactions with family and school environments." (p. 100) However, the *Technology Content Standards* offer little if any guidance on how to identify such problems. The vignette provided on the following page of the *Standards,* "Can you Help Mike Mulligan?", is based on a literature connection rather than children's environments.

When children make maps, they are engaged in design. If the map is of the bedroom (see p. 105, figure 4-19), the first task is to decide what is important to show. For some the problem is one of how to show both horizontal and vertical surfaces at the same time, all around the room. Deciding how to represent the room is a design problem. Designing a map of the route from home to school is a similar design problem: How much of the space between home and school needs to be shown in order to communicate how to get from one place to another? What are the features it is essential to include? Throughout

Mapping you see children analyzing their environments and creating maps to represent them.

Where does technology education "fit" in the existing curriculum? The Technology Standards address this problem by claiming that technology can enhance other disciplines: "Perhaps the most surprising message of the *Technology Content Standards* … is the role technological studies can play in students' learning of other subjects." (p. 6) We support this claim in the following sections, which draw the connections between *Stuff That Works!* and national standards in science, math, English language arts, and social studies.

Benchmarks for Science Literacy

There are two primary standards documents for science education: The American Association for the Advancement of Science (AAAS) *Benchmarks for Science Literacy* (1993) and the National Research Council (NRC) *National Science Education Standards* (1996). Unlike the *National Science Education Standards,* the *Benchmarks* provide explicit guidance for math, technology, and social science education, as well as science. The *Benchmarks* draw heavily on a previous AAAS report, *Science for All Americans* (1989), which is a statement of goals and general principles rather than a set of standards. *Benchmarks* recast the general principles of *Science for All Americans* (SFAA) as minimum performance objectives at each grade level.

The performance standards in *Benchmarks* are divided among 12 chapters. These include three generic chapters regarding the goals and methods of science, math and technology; six chapters providing major content objectives for the physical, life, and social sciences; technology and mathematics; and three generic chapters dealing with the history of science, "common themes," and "habits of mind." The last four chapters of *Benchmarks* provide supporting material, such as a glossary of terms and references to relevant research.

Recognizing that standards are necessary but not sufficient for education reform, the AAAS has also developed some supplementary documents to support the process of curriculum change. These include *Resources for Science Literacy: Professional Development* (1997), which suggests reading materials for teachers, presents outlines of relevant teacher education courses, and provides comparisons between the *Benchmarks,* the Math Standards, the Science Standards and the Social Studies Standards. A subsequent publication, *Blueprints for Science Reform* (1998) offers guidance for changing the education infrastructure to support science, math, and technology education reform. The recommendations in *Blueprints* are directed towards administrators, policy makers, parent and community groups, researchers, teacher educators, and industry groups. A subsequent AAAS document, *Designs for Science Literacy* (2001), provides examples of curriculum initiatives that are based on standards.

The *Benchmarks* present a compelling argument for technology education. The authors present the current situation in stark terms: "In the United States, unlike in most developed countries in the world, technology as a subject has largely been ignored in the schools." (p. 41) Then they point out the importance of technology in children's lives, its omission from the curriculum notwithstanding: "Young children are veteran technology users by the time they enter school…. [They] are also natural explorers and inventors, and they like to make things." (p. 44) To resolve this contradiction, "School should give students many opportunities to examine the properties of materials, to use tools, and to design and build things." (p. 44).

Like the Technology *Standards,* the *Benchmarks* identify design as a key process of technology and advocate strongly for first-hand experience in this area. "Perhaps the best way to become familiar with the nature of engineering and design is to do some." (p. 48) As children become engaged in design, they "begin to enjoy challenges that require them to clarify a problem, generate criteria for an acceptable solution, try one out, and then make adjustments or start over again with a newly proposed solution." (p. 49) These statements strongly support the basic approach of *Stuff That Works!,* which is to engage children in analysis and design activities based on the technologies already familiar to them.

Like *Stuff That Works!,* the *Benchmarks* also recognize the back-and-forth nature of design processes, which rarely proceed in a linear, predictable sequence from beginning to end.

In the chapter "Common Themes," *Benchmarks* identifies several "big ideas" that recur frequently in science, mathematics, and technology, and are powerful tools for explanation and design. Two of these themes, **systems** and **models,** are at least as important in technology as in science, and both are squarely addressed by *Mapping.* The section on systems begins, "One of the essential components of higher-order thinking is the ability to think about a whole in terms of the sum of its parts and, alternatively, about parts in terms of how they relate to one another and to the whole." (p. 262) The section goes on to point out that these ideas are difficult, and learned only through studying progressively more complex examples. *Mapping* provides a sequence of activities that provide experience in using higher order thinking skills that relate parts to wholes and vice-versa. The activities begin with children representing things as simple as a chalk box and progress to where they can represent their desks in relation to all the other things in the room.

Another of the common themes is models, which are "tools for learning about the things they are meant to resemble." These include mathematical and conceptual models, as well as physical models. Maps are models of the areas they represent. They can be two or three dimensional. They can be constructed to scale or not to scale. For the map-maker, the map is a way of encoding information about the area being represented, and through that process gain a greater understanding of the space being represented.

Map-making is a technology that depends on, and develops, mathematical skills, particularly skills of measurement, geometry, and spatial relations. *Benchmarks,* in the chapter "The Mathematical World," describes these goals for grades 6 through 8:

Learning to find locations in reality and on maps using rectangular and polar coordinates can contribute to an understanding of scale and illustrate one of the important connections between numbers and geometry. Shape in these grades is strongly related to spatial measurements. Students should have extensive experience in measuring and estimating perimeter, area, volume, and angles, choosing appropriate measurement units and measuring tools. As much as possible, these activities should be carried out in the context of actual projects, that is, in order to design and build something. (p. 244)

Mapping activities address these goals time and again. The process of locating your own desk in relation to other things in the classroom stimulates repeated measurements, the use of coordinates, and grappling with the concepts of scale. These processes can be seen in teacher stories in Chapter 4, particularly the stories of Felice Piggott, Angel Gonzalez, and Michael Gatton.

The importance of learning by doing is stressed in the chapter called "Habits of Mind." The section on "Manipulation and Observation" states, "Education for science literacy implies that students be helped to develop the habit of using tools, along with scientific and mathematical ideas and computation skills, to solve practical problems…" As they attempt to map different areas, whether their own bedrooms, the routes from home to school, or furniture arrangements in classroom or cafeteria, students find it necessary to collect data and make judgments based on evidence, not opinion. These analysis and design activities lead to important "habits of mind": "By the end of second grade, students should raise questions about the world around them and be willing to seek answers to some of them by making careful observations and trying things out." (p. 285) By comparing one another's maps and assessing whether they make sense, they develop "critical response skills": "By the end of second grade, students should ask 'How do you know?' in appropriate situations and attempt reasonable answers when others ask them the same question." (p. 298)

The uses of symbols, graphics, and models for communication are a recurring theme of *Benchmarks.* "Communication" appears as a major category under "The Designed World"; it reappears as "Symbolic

Relationships" under "The Mathematical World," as one of the "Common Themes," and as one of the "Habits of Mind." As we shall discuss in greater detail in the section on the *Standards for the English Language Arts,* all of the ***Stuff That Works!*** topics integrate communication as a central activity. Furthermore, *Mapping* focuses specifically on the analysis and design of techniques for representing and communicating information.

Mapping presents map-making as a way of communicating ideas and information about the arrangement of objects in space. Students make their own maps and then test them to see how well they correspond to the territory mapped. *Benchmarks* advocates these sorts of activities in the following terms: "Students also can begin to compare their objects, drawings and constructions to the things they portray or resemble." (p. 268) Similarly, this ability is specified under "Communication Skills": "By the end of second grade, students should be able to draw pictures that correctly portray at least some features of the thing being described." (p. 296)

Mapping engages children in developing and using drawings and symbols to communicate information. The *Benchmarks* section on "Communication" in "The Designed World" recommends just these sorts of activities:

Young children are fascinated by the various forms of giving messages, including sign language, road signs, recycling symbols, and company logos, and they should

have opportunities to invent forms of their own. Their symbols can be used in classroom routines, illustrating the need to have common meanings for signs, symbols and gestures. They should learn that writing things down and drawing pictures could help them tell their ideas to others accurately.... Students can discuss what the best ways are to convey different kinds of messages – not to decide the right answers, of course, but to start thinking about advantages and disadvantages. (p. 197)

The section on "Communication Skills" specifies mapping types of activities in a different context: "By the end of fifth grade, students should be able to write instructions that others can follow in carrying out a procedure [and] make sketches to aid in explaining procedures or ideas." (p. 296)

The National Science Education Standards

In 1991, the National Science Teachers Association asked the National Research Council to develop a set of national science education standards. These standards were intended to complement the *Benchmarks,* which include math, technology, and social studies as well as natural science. The National Research Council (NRC) includes the National Academy of Sciences, which is composed of the most highly regarded scientists in the country. Over the course of the next five years, the NRC involved thousands

of scientists, educators, and engineers in an extensive process of creating and reviewing drafts of the new science standards. The results were published in 1996 as the *National Science Education Standards* (NSES).

Who is the audience for standards? The conventional view is that standards outline what students should know and be able to do, and that teachers are accountable for assuring that their students meet these guidelines. The NSES take a much broader approach, looking at the whole range of systemic changes needed to reform science education. The document is organized into six sets of standards. Only one of the six, the "Science Content Standards," talks directly about what children should learn through science education. The other five address other components of the education infrastructure, including classroom environments, teaching methods, assessment, professional development, administrative support at the school and district levels, and policy at the local, state, and national levels.

Collectively, these standards outline the roles of a large group of people on whom science education depends: teachers, teacher educators, staff developers, curriculum developers, designers of assessments, administrators, superintendents, school board members, politicians, informed citizens, and leaders of professional associations. If an administrator or school board member were to ask a teacher, "What are you doing to address the *National Science Education Standards?*" the teacher would be fully justified in responding, "What are you doing to meet them?" One message that recurs frequently in the NSES is that teachers must be regarded as professionals, with a vital stake in the improvement of science education and an active role "in the ongoing planning and development of the school science program." (p. 50) More specifically, they should "participate in decisions concerning the allocation of time and other resources to the science program" (p. 51). The *Standards* explicitly reject the reduction of teachers to technicians or functionaries who carry out somebody else's directives. "Teachers must be acknowledged and treated as professionals whose work requires understanding and ability." The organization of schools must change too: "School leaders must structure and sustain suitable support systems for the work that teachers do" (p. 223).

Teachers should also play a major role in deciding and/or designing the science curriculum. The *Standards* call for teachers to "select science content and adapt and design curricula to meet the needs, interests, abilities and experiences of students." Although teachers set the curriculum initially, they should remain flexible: "Teaching for understanding requires responsiveness to students, so activities and strategies are continuously adapted and refined to address topics arising from student inquiries and experiences, as well as school, community and national events." (p. 30) Not only teachers, but also students, should play a major role in curriculum planning. The Teaching Standards make this point explicit: "Teachers [should] give students the opportunity to participate in setting

goals, planning activities, assessing work and designing the environment." (p. 50)

The Science Standards do not make the distinction between design and inquiry as sharply as do the Technology Standards: "Children in grades K-4 understand and can carry out design activities earlier than they can inquiry activities, but they cannot easily tell the difference between the two, nor is it important whether they can." (p.135) Thus, many of the abilities and concepts needed to meet the standard "Science as Inquiry" are also developed through design. These include: "Ask a question about objects… in the environment"; "plan and conduct a simple investigation"; "employ simple equipment and tools to gather data"; and "communicate investigations or explanations." (p. 122)

Mapping provides many opportunities to develop these inquiry abilities. Even young children are interested in representing where things are in their environment. They become fascinated observing and drawing objects from different perspectives, as Annette found with her kindergarten class.

Felice's fifth-graders enjoyed the challenge of figuring out how to represent classroom space and furniture to scale, then collecting the data to do so. As children in this class discovered, the ability to map spaces can lead directly into planning the improvement of spaces. The NSES "Teaching Standards" say this is where we should be leading them. As part of challenging students to take responsibility for their learning, teachers [should] involve them in the design and management of the learning environ-

ment. Even the youngest students can and should participate in discussions and decisions about using time and space for work. (p. 45)

Principles and Standards for School Mathematics

The first of the major standards documents, *Curriculum and Evaluation Standards for School Mathematics,* was published in 1989 by the National Council of Teachers of Mathematics (NCTM). Additional standards for teaching and assessment were published in 1991 and 1995, respectively. In 2000, the NCTM released a new document, *Principles and Standards for School Mathematics,* intended to update and consolidate the classroom-related portions of the three previous documents. Some of the major features of the new volume, different from the prior version, are the addition of the Principles, the division of the standards into the categories "Content" and "Process," and the inclusion of a new process standard called "Representation."

The new NCTM document acknowledges the limitations of educational standards: "Sometimes the changes made in the name of standards have been superficial or incomplete… Efforts to move in the direction of the original NCTM Standards are by no means fully developed or firmly in place." (pp. 5-6) In spite of this candid assessment, the authors remain optimistic about the future impact of standards. Their goal is to provide a common framework for curriculum developers and teachers nationwide. If all schools follow the same standards, then teachers will be able to assume that "students will reach certain levels of conceptual understanding and procedural fluency by certain points in the curriculum." (p. 7)

The NCTM *Principles and Standards* begin by presenting the six sets of principles, which are the underlying assumptions for the standards. Some of these principles are common to the other standards documents: that there should be high expectations of all students, that the goal of learning is deep understanding, and that assessment should be integrated with curriculum. Other principles underscore the need to learn from cognitive research. More than in any other field, there has been extensive research into how students learn mathematics, and this research base is reflected in the *Principles*. For example, the "Curriculum Principle" calls for coherent sets of lessons, focused collectively on one "big idea." Similarly, the "Teaching Principle" specifies that teachers must be aware of students' cognitive development. The "Learning Principle" cites research on how learning can be most effective.

The standards themselves are organized into two categories: Content Standards and Process Standards. The former describe what students should learn, in the areas of Number and Operations, Algebra, Geometry, Measurement, and Data Analysis and Probability. The Process Standards discuss how students should acquire and make use of the content knowledge. The subcategories are Problem Solving, Reasoning and Proof, Communication, Connections, and Representation. Unlike the earlier NCTM document, the new version uses all the same standards across all of the grade levels, from K through 12. In this way, the NCTM is advocating for a carefully structured curriculum, which builds upon and extends a few fundamental ideas systematically across the grades. Readers may be surprised to find an Algebra Standard for grades K-2, or a Number and Operations Standard for grades 9-12.

Stuff That Works! units and activities offer rich opportunities for fulfilling a key ingredient of the NCTM standards: learning and using mathematics in context. The Process Standard called "Connections" makes it clear that mathematics should be learned by using it to solve problems arising from "other subject areas and disciplines" as well as from students' daily lives." (p. 66) *Stuff That Works!* fulfills this standard in two fundamental respects: it provides mathematics connections with another subject area, technology, and it uses artifacts and issues from everyday life as the source of material for study. The mathematics students learn is drawn from all of the Content Standards, as well as all of the Process Standards except for Reasoning and Proof.

Mapping has some of the most obvious connections with mathematics. In the earliest mapping activities, a young child develops an awareness of numbers by counting objects on a desk, and then constructing a map that shows the same number of symbols as objects. This is an example of learning to "count with understanding and recognize 'how many' in sets of objects" (p. 78), a basic ingredient of the Number and Operations Standard for grades K-2. As children's mapping skills progress they learn to arrange things on the map according to their arrangements in real space. In so doing, they develop the basic techniques of "visualization, spatial reasoning and geometric modeling" (p. 43) that are central to the Geometry Standard. Another example is the effort to "recognize and represent shapes from different perspectives" (p. 96), which are among the early mapping activities. Mapping also provides natural ways of meeting the Representation Standard, as children develop their own ways of representing geometric arrangements; and the Communication Standard, as they present these maps to one another to interpret.

By mapping to scale, students in the upper elementary grades develop an intuitive sense of ratio and proportion, a key ingredient of the Number and Operations Standard for grades 6-8. Making a scale map involves a considerable amount of measurement, using standard and/or non-standard units, and appropriate tools, as specified in the Measurement Standard. The work on visualization and spatial relationships becomes more complex, as students work on maps from a "bird's-eye view" as well as from other perspectives. Similarly, they develop greater facility with representation as they develop their own symbols to represent things on a map. Their maps also become powerful tools for communication, as students use them to convey information about routes to follow and about the results of scientific experiments. As others try to interpret and use their maps, the deficiencies become obvious. The need to revise and refine a map to make it more useful is a natural occasion for meeting the Problem Solving Standard

The activities in *Mapping* also offer powerful opportunities for developing the basic themes of the Representation Standard, which reject the memorization of symbols and their use as "ends in themselves." Instead, "Representations should be treated as essential elements in supporting students' understanding of mathematical concepts and relationships; in communicating mathematical approaches, arguments and understandings to one's self and others; in recognizing connections among related mathematical concepts; and in applying mathematics to realistic problem situations through modeling." (p. 67) In *Mapping,* students develop map legends. They invent a wide variety of symbols to represent everyday environmental features. These are tested when maps are put to the test of communicating information to other map-readers. These experiences provide the background for the use of symbols, including graphic representations, in mathematics.

Mapping involves students in developing ways to represent their own immediate environments. In the course

of mapping activities, they have to decide what kind of data to collect, how to organize it, and how to represent it in the two dimensional world of maps. This process of data collection, organization and representation is advocated by the NCTM:

The Data Analysis and Probability Standard recommends that students formulate questions that can be answered using data and addresses what is involved in gathering and using data wisely. Students should learn how to collect data, organize their own or others' data, and display the data in graphs or charts that will be useful in answering their questions. This Standard also includes learning some methods for analyzing data and some ways for making inferences and conclusions from data. (p. 48)

Standards for the English Language Arts

By 1991, it had become clear that standards would be produced for all of the major school subjects. Fearful that English language standards might be produced without a firm basis in research and practice, two major professional organizations requested Federal funding for their own standards effort. The following year, the Department of Education awarded a grant for this purpose to the Center for the Study of Reading at the University of Illinois, which agreed to work closely with the

two organizations, the National Council of Teachers of English (NCTE) and the International Reading Association (IRA). This effort culminated in the 1996 publication of the *Standards for the English Language Arts* by the NCTE and IRA. These ELA Standards are now widely accepted for their clear, concise outline of English language education.

The ELA Standards adopt an unusually comprehensive view of "literacy," much broader in its scope than the traditional definition of "knowing how to read and write," or the earlier one of "the ability to read and write one's own name." (p. 4) Literacy also includes the ability to think critically, and encompasses oral and visual, as well as written communication. Recognizing that these forms of language "are often given limited attention in the curriculum," the *Standards* outline the variety of means used to convey messages in contemporary society:

Being literate in contemporary society means being active, critical, and creative users not only of print and spoken language, but also of the visual language of film and television, commercial and political advertising, photography, and more. Teaching students how to interpret and create visual texts such as illustrations, charts, graphs, electronic displays, photographs, film and video is another essential component of the English language arts curriculum. (pp. 5-6)

According to the ELA *Standards*, there are three major aspects to language learning: **content, purpose,** and **development.** Content standards address only *what* students should learn, but not why or how: "knowledge alone is of little value if one has no need to—or cannot—apply it." The *Standards* identify four purposes for learning and using language: "for obtaining and communicating information, for literary response and expression, for learning and reflection, and for problem solving and application." (p. 16) Purpose also figures prominently in the third dimension of language learning, development, which describes how students acquire this facility. "We learn language not simply for the sake of learning language; we learn it to make sense of the world around us and to communicate our understanding with others." (p. 19)

Of course, purpose and motivation vary from one situation to another. The authors of the *Standards* make this point, too, in their discussion of "context." "Perhaps the most obvious way in which language is social is that it almost always relates to others, either directly or indirectly: we speak to others, listen to others, write to others, read what others have written, make visual representations to others and interpret their visual representations." Language development proceeds through the practice of these communication skills with others: "We become participants in an increasing number of language groups that necessarily influence the ways in which we speak, write and

represent." While language development is primarily social, there is an individual dimension as well: "All of us draw on our own sets of experiences and strategies as we use language to construct meaning from what we read, write, hear, say, observe, and represent." (p. 22)

How does this broad conception of literacy and its development relate to daily classroom practice? The authors recognize that the ELA *Standards* may be in conflict with the day-to-day demands placed on teachers. "They may be told they should respond to the need for reforms and innovations while at the same time being discouraged from making their instructional practices look too different from those of the past." Among those traditional practices are the use of standardized tests, "which often focus on isolated skills rather than contextualized learning." Prescribed texts and rigid lesson plans are further barriers to reform, because they tend to preclude "using materials that take advantage of students' interests and needs" and replace "authentic, open-ended learning experiences" (p. 7). Another problem is "the widespread practice of dividing the class day into separate periods [which] precludes integration among the English language arts and other subject areas" (p. 8). Taken seriously, these standards would lead to wholesale reorganization of most school experiences.

This introductory material sets the stage for the twelve content standards, which define "what students should know and be able to do in the English language arts." (p. 24) Although these are labeled "content" standards,

"content cannot be separated from the purpose, development and context of language learning." (p. 24) In a variety of ways, the twelve standards emphasize the need to engage students in using language clearly, critically and creatively, as participants in "literacy communities." Within these communities, students sometimes participate as *receivers* of language—by interpreting graphics, reading and listening and—and sometimes as *creators*—by using visual language, writing, and speaking.

Some teachers have used the *Stuff That Works!* activities and units primarily to promote language literacy, rather than for their connections with math or science. Technology activities offer compelling reasons for children to communicate their ideas in written, spoken, and visual form. In early childhood and special education classrooms, teachers have used *Stuff That Works!* to help children overcome difficulties in reading and writing, because it provides natural and non-threatening entry points for written expression. In the upper elementary grades, *Stuff That Works!* activities offer rich opportunities for students to want to use language for social purposes. Several characteristics of *Stuff That Works!* contribute to its enormous potential for language learning and use:

- Every unit begins with an extensive group discussion of what terms mean, how they apply to particular examples, how to categorize things, and/or what problems are most important.

- The activities focus on artifacts and problems that engage children's imaginations, making it easy to communicate about them. Teachers who use *Stuff That Works!* usually require students to record their activities and reflections in journals.
- This guide, along with *Signs, Symbol, and Codes,* focuses on the problem of communication and offers numerous experiences in visual thinking and visual communication.
- The activities in *Mapping* engage students in representing their own classrooms, schools, and neighborhoods. These endeavors require extensive use of language in a group setting to accomplish purposes of real importance to the children.

For each of the *Stuff That Works!* topics, the opening activity is a scavenger hunt or brainstorming session. In a scavenger hunt, students develop an understanding of the topic by collecting and examining physical examples and discussing them. Often there are debates about how well some of the examples fit the category. For example, Minerva Rivera's fourth-graders had brought in newspaper clippings that they considered maps. In the course of the discussion, one student reported, "My group doesn't think a cartoon is a map. It doesn't show you where to go." This statement led to arguments and

counter-arguments about what constitutes a "map." Minerva's students were beginning to "participate as knowledgeable, reflective, creative and critical members" of a literacy community. (ELA Standard # 11, p. 44)

Two of the *Stuff That Works!* guides, *Mapping* and *Signs, Symbols, and Codes,* focus specifically on visual communication. Students learn to interpret and evaluate examples of graphic communication created by others, and they also create and test their own designs. These kinds of experiences in visual communication are rarely encountered in most school curricula, although mandated by the ELA Standards. The design of signs, symbols, and maps engages children very directly in basic issues of language and communication, because the territory is less well-defined than written and spoken languages and therefore more open to innovation and discussion.

For example, in Felice Piggott's fifth-grade class, each student had to create a map showing others the route to follow from one point in the classroom to another. These maps could only work if they used conventions shared by both mapmaker and audience. For a map to be effective, both reader and writer have to concur about what the symbols mean. The test of such a design is obvious: can the reader figure out what it means?

Curriculum Standards for Social Studies

The social studies encompass a variety of disciplines, all concerned with the complex and changing relationships between the individual and society. Some of these fields have traditionally been taught as separate subjects. By the early 1990's major standards-setting efforts were underway for civics, economics, geography, and history. In an effort to provide a framework for these separate disciplinary standards, the National Council for the Social Studies (NCSS) issued Expectations of Excellence: Curriculum Standards for Social Studies in 1994. This document is not intended to replace the individual disciplinary standards, but rather to serve as a guide for integrating them under broad interdisciplinary themes. "Teachers and curriculum designers are encouraged first to establish their program frameworks using the social studies standards as a guide, then to use individual sets of standards from history, geography, civics, economics, or other disciplines to guide the development of strands and courses within their programs." (p. 17)

According to the NCSS, a primary purpose of social studies is to prepare students for their roles as citizens in a democratic society. "NCSS has recognized the importance of educating students … who are able to use knowledge about their community, nation, and world, along with skills of data collection and analysis, collaboration, decision-making, and problem-solving

[for] shaping our future and sustaining and improving our democracy." (p. 3)

This statement covers a lot of ground, and supports both sides of a major political controversy over the role of social studies in the schools. Should students learn what their society wants them to know, or should they develop as critical thinkers who can improve the way the society works? The NCSS Standards say "yes" on both counts: students should not only become "committed to the ideas and values" of our society, but also learn "decision-making and problem-solving." A companion NCSS document, *National Standards for Teaching Social Studies* (1997) is even more explicit: "Social studies teachers should … encourage student development of critical thinking." (p.35)

What sorts of educational strategies will accomplish these goals? The Social Studies Standards outline five basic "Principles of Teaching and Learning." To begin with, these should be "meaningful": "Students learn connected networks of knowledge, skills, beliefs and attitudes that they will find useful both in and out of school." Learning should "integrate across the curriculum," using "authentic activities that call for real-life applications." In applying what they have learned, stu-

dents should "make value-based decisions" and develop a "commitment to social responsibility." (pp. 11-12) The Teaching Standards set the context for such education, in calling for "learning environments that encourage social interaction, active engagement in learning and self-motivation." (NCSS, 1997, p. 35)

Mapping offers these sorts of opportunities. In mapping activities, students begin with challenges of real interest to them: how to represent my bedroom and the important things in it, or how to show my route to school so someone else could follow it. The map-making experience integrates the skills of many curricular areas, Social Studies, Mathematics, and English are the most obvious. Children engage with one another as they try to figure out what the other's map depicts. Even closer collaboration is demanded when each is responsible for a piece of a larger map.

APPENDIX

A Mapping Unit in Special Education

Mary Flores teaches in a special education resource room in Community Elementary School (C.E.S) 42 in the South Bronx. Over the course of the day she teaches 32 bilingual second- through fifth-graders, three quarters of whom read at or below first-grade level. Mary has many years' experience in teaching inquiry-based science, in leading teacher workshops, and in mentoring less experienced teachers. In the resource room her major task is to improve children's reading. She uses work in science and technology as a major stimulant to develop their skills in English language arts.

In this appendix, we are reproducing an extended narrative of her work. It handles most of the topics discussed in Chapter 4, "Stories." More significantly, it reflects Mary's thinking as she tried a variety of approaches with her bilingual special education students. She records her own creative process as she tries things that don't work, re-assesses them, and thinks of new ways of starting. Mary's narrative also captures the dialogue of the students as they grapple with the material.

September 12

The beginning of a new school year. The beginning of a new start. But, where do I start? We have been in school a little more than a week. I spent last week assessing students who are at risk of failure. By the end of the week I had assessed a total of thirty-two second to fifth grade students. Twenty-four of the students scored at or below a first grade level! You can imagine the task that lies ahead of me. This brings me to my concerns. Where do I begin? How do I integrate reading and mapping? I'm excited by the curriculum and I want to do the best that I can. But, I also have to keep in mind that there is a lot of work to do in order to help these students become better readers.

September 14

This weekend I developed a plan. First, I had to schedule the students. As the resource room teacher I remediate eight students at a time. At first, I thought I would group by grade. Although, I generally don't group homogeneously, I decided to go this route. It would make my job easier.

Once my scheduling dilemma was accomplished, I began "mapping" out a curriculum. The ideas came quickly, but I still didn't know where to begin. I needed reassurance. I spoke to colleagues who helped me through my insecurities. Now I'm excited about beginning the week.

September 15

I arrived at school early and posted all types of maps around the room:

- subway maps
- bus maps
- a world map
- a topographical map showing land forms
- a map of the United States
- a map of the 5 boroughs

I led the first group in a discussion about maps and mapping. The discussion centered around the maps that were posted around the room:

- They give you directions.
- They tell you where the states are.
- They tell you how to get somewhere when you get lost.

I handed out graphic organizers (based on the K,W,L model). I asked them to list everything they knew about mapping, what they wanted to know about mapping and how they would go about answering their questions.

September 18

I decided to jump right into mapping the classroom. Last night while searching through my library I came across a gold mine! My son (who is away) left behind a schematic of a generator. I knew this was the key to redirecting the student's thoughts regarding mapping. They had probably never seen a map like this.

I opened the lesson by showing my first group (fourth- and fifth-graders) the schematic of the generator. "What is this?" I asked. "A map of the school. See the numbers. They are the numbers on the doors of the classrooms!" commented Patrick. Other suggestions: the park, Ms. Flores' kitchen, the schoolyard, and a computer. I did not tell the group what the schematic was. I didn't want to make the mistake of giving them too many answers. Additionally, if I told them it was the map of a generator it would mean nothing to them.

I followed this initial lesson with a story. It's amazing, but the idea came to me five minutes before the group entered the room. I told the groups, "At night when you are asleep, friendly ghouls, goblins, and ghosts enter this classroom in order to read all the books in our library. However, they keep bumping into the furniture. Every morning I have to come in and rearrange the furniture. Last night, they left a note in the typewriter which said, 'Dear Ms. Flores, Please have your class make maps of your classroom so that we won't keep bumping in to the furniture. Thank you, The Monsters.' Of course students asked, "Ms. Flores, are you telling the truth!" "You're just saying that to scare us," said Nicole. I assured them that it was a true story.

I gave them a quick lesson on the use of a key and the use of symbols to represent the furniture. I put out different sized graph paper and instructed them to make the map.

I modeled for the students by engaging in the activity. Students watched as I used the squares on the floor to make my map.

Patrick was curious about what I was doing and he came over to see. I didn't tell him what I was doing, but he figured it out. He then went over and got the schematic of the generator to use as a model. He and Christian used this model to make their maps. It was not what I had expected. I thought someone in the class would follow my lead. They didn't.

Moises and Heriberto made drawings, while Nicole and Shelva used the mini-stampers to make the maps. I noticed that Christina began with the key. But, the symbols didn't match the map. None of the maps showed accurate representations of the classroom.

Did I expect too much? Did I move too quickly? I know I moved too quickly by introducing the use of symbols as a representation. I have to consider what the next step will be.

Although the maps were not what I'd expected, the students were totally engaged in the activity. The activity was not a failure. These maps served as a pre-test. Let's see what they will be able to do in a few weeks. My expectations for the students are high. I expect that with more structured guidance, they will be able to make accurate maps. Should I move out of the classroom to give them a change? I don't know. I'll have to think about that one.

I decided to try something different with my last group, The Incredible Hulks (second- and third-graders). This was the lesson I had initially planned for today. I read the book *The Very Lonely Firefly* by Eric Carle. I chose this book because it lends itself to story mapping. I read the book to the group, then I instructed them to make a story map of the route the firefly followed. I gave them adding machine tape to use for their maps. The students were engaged in the activity. In fact, I had a difficult time getting them to stop. I will follow up this activity by having the students write about their illustrations. In this way, I integrate skills, which need remediation.

September 22

This weekend I had time to reflect on the past week. I realized that I moved too quickly. The use of symbols to represent objects was much too complex (for now). With that in mind, I decided to go back to the "mapping" board. I revisited the mapping games and decided to do the "Finding Shapes" activity. I made up a worksheet.

I motivated the class by asking a question, "Where do you usually see pigeons?" Responses included: on top of buildings, on top of houses, on trees, in windows. I led them to the idea that pigeons converge in high places. I asked, "If a bird were to enter this classroom, where do you think he would be the happiest?" Christina said, "I know the answer to this question. It would be the light because it is the highest."

I directed the students to a rectangle, which I made using masking tape. Inside of the rectangle, I had randomly placed blocks of different shapes and colors. (See Figure A-1.) I began the lesson by asking students to stand around the square. "Pretend you are a bird. Look down on our classroom and name the shapes you see." Students said, "circle, sphere, rectangle, rectangular prism, triangle, parallelogram."

A-1: **Identifying shapes from a bird's-eye view**

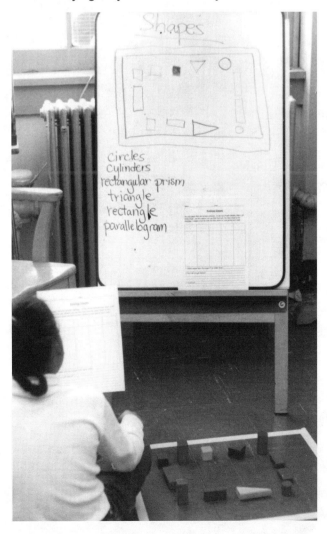

I directed the students to the rectangle I had drawn on the dry eraser board. I asked Nicole to point to one of the blocks on the floor. "What shape is it?" Initially, she said it was a cylinder. I then informed all of the students that they were looking at only the top. Nicole looked at the shape again and answered, "A circle." I asked her to tell me "where on the map I would draw the shape." She pointed to the proper place on the map. I asked the same question of each of the students in turn.

I used markers that corresponded to the colors of the blocks, so the students could visually see that the map on the dry eraser board was exactly like the one on the floor. Finally, I challenged them to find as many shapes as they could in the classroom all along reminding them that they were seeing objects from a bird's eye view. (Figure A-2, Finding Shapes, is the worksheet for this activity.)

The students eased through the activity. All the groups had similar experiences. The groups that had difficulty with the task were my non-readers/writers. However, Teashannon and Julio solved the problem by immediately going to *The New Oxford Picture Dictionary* by E.C. Parmwell to spell unknown words. This dictionary categorizes objects by groups. Each picture is labeled with a number. Students refer to the number and it gives them the spelling. Julio and Teashannon were able to find the chapter on the classroom. This facilitated their writing.

Today was a very productive day. I accomplished what I set out to do. I know that the students have a better understanding of how to map. I realize that I have to introduce concepts in little bits.

A-2: "Finding shapes" worksheet

Name: ChristianRobinson **Date** Sept 23, 1997

Finding Shapes

On your paper there are several columns. At the top of each column, draw a different shape. List any objects you can find that have the same shape as the drawings. Compare your list with the lists others in your group have made.

○	□	▢	▭	▢
Globe	Window	door	Bookshelf	white board
Clock	floor	Bathroom	lights	cinder lar
Sphere	charkboard	calinder	flag	poster
Beanbag	map	pencil	toster	
pole	dest	cup	hoven	
bucket	computer frame	picture frame	Author study	
behind door	puppet box			

1. Which shapes have the longest lists under them? rectangle because mosly every thing in her is rectangle
2. How did you get started? first thing I thought about is the circle because it is the hardest thing to find.
3. Questions? who invented maps?

September 23

Some students continued to work on finding shapes. I discussed with each group the three main shapes we had found in the room: circle, square, and rectangle. I had them read from their lists and I wrote their responses on chart paper. This chart will be posted in the room for reference.

William seemed to have reached his frustration level with the finding shapes activity. He has difficulty writing, so this activity was a challenge for him. I knew I needed to redirect his focus. I asked William if he liked building with blocks. He said that he did and I asked if he could build. I informed him that he needed to have a partner in order to build. He chose to work with LisMarie.

They were assigned the task of building a structure for the miniature toys found in the toy box. I gave them a worksheet and set an area for them to work in. Afterwards, I told them to map the design. Again, I made a mistake. The structure they built was complex, thereby hampering their efforts to make an accurate representation. Back to the "mapping" board.

September 25

New plan. I told the students a new story. "The miniature animals, cars, and people need a structure. You will use blocks, Legos, or gogoolplexes to build a structure. Since these toys are miniature, you will only use the space on your desk. Afterwards you will map your design on the worksheet and you will answer the questions."

The students were totally engaged in the activity. This allowed me to observe what each child was doing. Moises and Derrell decided to make the "blueprint" first. I wonder whether this was because they both possess artistic abilities. They were the only ones that chose to approach the activity in this manner. Victoria was not content with the blocks on her table. She kept grabbing blocks directly from Cynthia's structure. This led to a discussion on sharing and working together.

Since space was limited, the structures were not very complex. I knew it would be easier for them to map their design. Most of the drawings resembled the actual structures. At least they were thinking about shapes and perspective. Some chose to draw the structure from an aerial view. Others sat and mapped their design, thereby getting a different perspective. I sat with individual children to help them answer the questions, as well

as to prompt them in order to get them to explain their answers. Some of the students did not get to finish. We will continue this activity for as long as the students want to revisit it.

What a wonderful turn of events!

An anecdote: Prior to this activity, I had shared with another teacher the worktime journal process questions. That individual told me that the questions were too complex. He did not believe they'd be able to answer them. Boy, was he wrong!

October 1

We revisited the mapping of the classroom activity yet a third time. I wanted to see if the "Finding Shapes" activity would help the students to see the room from a different perspective. Prior to this activity, I had labeled the room with directional signs, N, S, E, and W. I hoped the signs would make it easier for them to conceive of the room as a rectangle and, thus, translate it to paper. I called their attention to the directional signs and showed them on the compass how I determined the position of the signs.

Before beginning, I stressed that they should use only shapes to represent the furniture in the room. We reviewed the shapes found in the classroom. Once students began work, I was free to aid those who needed my help and to make observations. What I found interesting was that the students chose to view the room from different perspectives. In so doing, some of the maps had the furniture on the reverse side of their paper. This led to a discussion on perspective.

Another problem I noticed was that students seemed to be struggling with how large to represent the furniture on paper. I noticed that Cynthia's map was out of proportion. I asked Cynthia whether the desk is larger than the file cabinet. She responded with a "no." Then I pointed out that her map shows that the desk is larger than the file cabinet. I told her to use the directional signs as her point of reference. Size was a problem for many of the students.

I am not sure how to get them to represent size without introducing scale mapping. Is scale mapping a difficult concept for my students? Should I map the room to scale and have them fill in the missing pieces? Should I move into mapping the room three dimensionally (clay, blocks, boxes)? I need this vacation time to rethink the whole mapping thing.

October 6

I decided to try to have the students represent the room three-dimensionally using the blocks. I cordoned off a large area of the floor of the classroom using masking tape. I made the outline the same as the shape of the classroom. I allowed two children to work in the area at a time. Today a total of six students worked in this area. Because I see five groups throughout the day, I am unable to leave the structures from day to day. This hampered the activity because the students ran out of time.

I audiotaped the questions I asked and the responses. I also left the tape running while the groups worked. I wanted to see if there was dialogue among them as they worked.

They talked throughout the activity. This made it easier to evaluate what they were doing. Often, it is difficult for me to observe what is going on within the small groups. Some of the students are very needy and consume much of my time. Audiotaping and videotaping allow me not to miss those exchanges. Here is how I introduced the activity with Moises and Derrell:

TEACHER:
There is something here on the floor. Can you tell me what you think it is?

DERRELL:
I think it's an off limits map because, aah, the whole thing is messed up, and you know, and you can not go through it. So they're waiting until you like fix the whole place up so you can work on it.

MOISES:
It looks something like the surrounding of a map, east, south, north, west, because it has the signs on each corner just like a map.

TEACHER:
If that's a map, what is it a map of?

MOISES:
Hmm. Maybe a building, maybe a school, it could be anything.

DERRELL:
A house?

TEACHER:
Suppose I told you that it is a map of this room and the blocks are the furniture. What do you think happened to the furniture?

DERRELL:
The furniture got breaked down and everybody's waiting until everything gets to...

TEACHER:

Your job is to put this room together. The only thing the blocks represent is the furniture, desks, chairs, right. You decide which blocks will represent the furniture. I will let the tape run while you work. Then you will map out your design.

While I worked with other students, Moises and Derrell worked cooperatively. I was curious about what was going on and would walk over occasionally. I did not intervene, but just watched. The following excerpt shows that, as teachers, we sometimes assume children know more than they do:

DERRELL:

We forgot that table. We gonna take four cubes. As a matter of fact, two cubes. We put the desk right in front of the computer right here, where the desk and the computer is at.

MOISES:

Yeah, there's a desk right there. No, no. That's a bad idea. The desk is the cube and the squares are the chairs.

DERRELL:

The two squares are the chair and we gonna leave it like that, alright!

MOISES:

We need another desk right here.

DERRELL:

No, that's in the east! So those two chairs right there, are the. No! That's the north side! No this is the northeast.

DERRELL:

South. Yeah, northsouth, eastsouth. That would be eastsouth not northsouth. Cause if it was northsouth it would have been that way.

MOISES:

It would have been that way, yeah. So, let's see. Now we need another desk, two chairs?

DERRELL:

That would be east. That's where the blackboard's at.

The students continued working on the task until I called time. Throughout the construction they continued to talk about where the objects would go. At some point they began talking about measurements. I don't know how they determined what would be an inch or even if they used the ruler to figure out where my desk would go:

DERRELL:

...The beanbag's right there.

MOISES:

We can use one of these guys for.. (think he was referring to a ruler)

DERRELL:

Okay. We can put that right here. One inch. One inch from the bookcase right there. And one inch away from the...

MOISES:

Now we need the bathroom door. We have nothing for the bathroom door!

DERRELL:

Except for this. What we need is just one more block for that white board.

MOISES:

I have a good idea. Maybe we should do this. We should work on the outside first and then come in.

DERRELL:

That's what we're doing.

MOISES:

We're just building the outside and the inside and it's crazy.

DERRELL:

That'll be our door. We have to stand up to see how it's coming out so far.

MOISES:
Then, we should compare it to the room. A desk here, a desk there, two chairs, two chairs.

DERRELL:
We're missing one thing. We need another desk. We need two bookcases...

I then questioned them about the process before I allowed them to map out their design on paper.

TEACHER:
Where did you begin?

MOISES:
From the outside in.

TEACHER:
Which side did you begin with?

DERRELL:
We started with the tables at the front of this room. So, after the front of this whole room we started going for the outside.

I realized, after reviewing the tape, that Moises and Derrell incorporated some of the skills from the previous activities. For example, they were beginning to think about perspective. They also developed a plan as they worked. They worked and reworked their construction. This shows me that they are processing. Additionally, I provision for children by placing a variety of materials in the centers. The students are encouraged to use these materials.

Chapter 2

Arnheim, Rudolph. *Visual Thinking.* Berkeley: University of California Press, 1969.

A classic exposition of the importance of art and art education in stimulating and supporting cognitive development. The final chapter explores the similarities and differences between art and science.

Crampton, K. and Finney, M. *Collins CDT: Design and Communication.* London: Collins Educational, 1988.

This volume in the British Craft, Design and Technology (CDT) Series is a secondary level survey of graphic communication techniques. It offers a brief summary and examples of how graphics are used in science, engineering and business, and includes many valuable suggestions about technique.

Education Development Center, Inc. *Designing Spaces: Visualizing, Planning and Building.* Cambridge, MA: Education Development Center.

A volume in the series *Seeing and Thinking Mathematically in the Middle Grades.* This book supports the use of geometry in analyzing buildings and designing models. It provides detailed instructions, in both English and Spanish, for drawing and analyzing solid shapes, and relates them to architectural design.

Eriksen, Aase and Wintermute, Marjorie. *Students, Structures, Spaces: Activities in the Built Environment.*

An activity book intended to increase children's awareness and involvement with their environments. Many of the activities including sketching both indoor and outdoor spaces, with very helpful hints about measuring, drawing to scale, enlarging and analyzing both indoor and outdoor spaces.

Feldman, David. *Beyond Universals in Cognitive Development.* Norwood, NJ: Ablex Publishing Co., 1980.

A technical book on developmental psychology. Chapter 3 contains valuable and readable material on how children's conceptions of space develop, as revealed by the maps they draw.

Ferguson, Eugene. *Engineering and the Mind's Eye.* Cambridge, MA: MIT Press, 1993.

This very readable volume traces the history and importance of graphic images in engineering. It includes numerous historic sketches by engineers and inventors.

Frazee, Bruce and Guardia, William. *Helping Your Child with Maps and Globes.* Glenview, IL: Scott Foresman, 1994.

A workbook intended for the early elementary grades. It uses structured activities to teach concepts of direction, distance, scale and symbolism.

Goodnow, Jacqueline. *Children Drawing.* Cambridge, MA: Harvard University Press, 1977.

The author uses children's drawings to provide evidence of their cognitive development. One chapter explores how children come to adopt the map-making conventions of their culture.

Greenhood, David. *Mapping.* Chicago: University of Chicago Press, 1964.

A classic introduction to the lore and techniques of mapping. It still provides a lot of useful background information about a wealth of topics, including direction finding, surveying, projections, relief maps, mapping equipment, and much more.

McKim, Robert. *Experiences in Visual Thinking* (Second Edition). Monterey, CA: Brooks/Cole Publishing Co., 1980.

McKim offers many exercises for exercising and improving one's visual thinking skills, as well as a thorough, non-technical account of the psychology of visual perception.

Mitchell, Lucy Sprague. *Young Geographers.* (Fourth Edition). New York: Bank Street College of Education, 1991.

Originally written in 1934, this classic work outlines the use of an inquiry method in geography. It offers many suggestions about including map-making and map-thinking at all levels of the K-12 curriculum.

Monmonier, Mark and Schnell, George. *Map Appreciation.* Englewood Cliffs, NJ: Prentice Hall, 1988.

Intended as a text for an introductory college geography course, this book focuses on the role and importance of maps in modern society. It also includes non-technical information on the elements of a map and the use of computers in mapping.

Monmonier, Mark. *How to Lie with Maps.* Chicago: University of Chicago Press, 1991.

This entertaining book was inspired by Darrell Huff's classic How to Lie with Statistics. The author provides abundant illustrations of how maps can be misleading inadvertently or for deliberate political or commercial purposes.

Monmonier, Mark. *Mapping It Out.* Chicago: University of Chicago Press, 1993.

A non-technical exposition on mapping techniques, intended for scholars in the humanities and social sciences. Many of the techniques could generate ideas for classroom use. The third chapter, "Visual Variables and Cartographic Symbols," is especially interesting.

Morrison, Philip and Phylis. *Powers of Ten: A Book About the Relative Size of Things in the Universe and the Effect of Adding Another Zero.* San Francisco: W.H. Freeman, 1982.

A classic, beautifully illustrated demonstration of how a simple image changes with scale factor.

Nelms, Henning. *Thinking with a Pencil.* Berkeley: Ten Speed Press, 1981.

An engaging, very readable "how-to" book for learning to illustrate. All kinds of drawing are included, and there are many examples of effective uses of graphics.

Taylor, Anne, Vlastos, George and Marshall, Alison. *Architecture and Children.* Seattle: Architecture and Children Institute, 1991.

An illustrated manual for both teachers and children that includes material on perspective drawing, floor plans, models, contour maps, and visual surveys.

Taylor, Barbara. *Maps and Mapping: Geography Facts and Experiments.* New York: Kingfisher Books, 1993.

A clearly written, well illustrated upper elementary level book. It includes inquiry activities related to bird's eye view, scale drawing, floor plans, contour maps and projections.

Tufte, Edward. *Envisioning Information.* Cheshire, CT: Graphics Press, 1990.

This beautifully illustrated work offers a wealth of ideas for "escaping flatland": putting multiple data dimensions on a page. Many of the examples are masterpieces of graphic design, and Tufte's commentary is equally illuminating.

U. S. Geological Survey. *What Do Maps Show?* Reston, VA: USGS, undated. Available free from the USGS at 1-800-USA MAPS.

This folder contains a poster and four lesson plans intended to teach basic map reading skills.

Weiss, Harvey. Maps: *Getting from Here to There.* Boston, Houghton Mifflin Co., 1991.

A book on map reading aimed at junior high school level, which includes basic information about scales, projections, and symbols.

Chapter 6

American Association for the Advancement of Science (1989). *Science for All Americans: A Project 2061 Report on Literacy Goals in Science, Mathematics and Technology.* Washington, DC: Author.

American Association for the Advancement of Science (1993). *Benchmarks for Science Literacy.* New York: Oxford University Press.

American Association for the Advancement of Science (1997). *Resources for Science Literacy.* New York: Oxford University Press.

American Association for the Advancement of Science (1998). *Blueprints for Reform.* New York: Oxford University Press.

American Association for the Advancement of Science (2001). *Designs for Science Literacy.* New York: Oxford University Press.

International Technology Education Association (1996). *Technology for All Americans: A Rationale and Structure for the Study of Technology.* Reston, VA: Author.

International Technology Education Association (2000). *Standards for Technological Literacy: Content for the Study of Technology.* Reston, VA: Author.

National Center on Education and the Economy (1997). *New Standards Performance Standards; Vol 1: Elementary School.* Washington, DC: Author.

National Council for the Social Studies (1994). *Expectations of Excellence: Curriculum Standards for Social Studies.* Washington, DC: Author.

National Council for the Social Studies (1997). *National Standards for Social Studies Teachers.* http://www.social studies.org/standards/teachers/standards.html

National Council of Teachers of English and International Reading Association (1996). *Standards for the English Language Arts.* Urbana, IL: Author.

National Council of Teachers of Mathematics (1989). *Curriculum and Evaluation Standards for School Mathematics.* Reston, VA: Author.

National Council of Teachers of Mathematics (2000). *Principles and Standards for School Mathematics.* Reston, VA: Author.

National Research Council (1996). *National Science Education Standards.* Washington, DC: National Academy Press.

Cardinal directions: The directions of the four chief points of the compass: north, south, east, and west.

Compass rose: A graphic symbol indicating the direction of north on a map; often an image of a compass needle, or arrow, pointing to north.

Coordinates on a map: A set of symbols placed along adjacent sides of a grid to identify the grid rows and columns; typically, alphabet letters are placed along the vertical side and numbers along the horizontal side.

Design: The creation of something new in order to solve a problem, and its evaluation to see how well it works.

Euclidian stage: Piaget's third stage of spatial development. It includes the abilities to handle coordinate systems, estimate distances, and interpret and produce maps to scale.

Geographical map: A two-dimensional representation of a portion of the earth's surface or of a space within a building.

Grid: A set of equally spaced, intersecting, horizontal and vertical lines. Superimposed on a map, a grid provides a way to specify a particular part of the map. It is the basis of a coordinate system.

Key: A table showing the translation of a set of graphic symbols into words that represent features in the area mapped; a map legend.

Orienting a map to a space: The process of aligning a map with the space it represents so that landmarks lie in the same direction from one's position on the map as they do from one's position in the real world.

Plan view: The perspective from directly above the object/space being viewed; the "bird's-eye" point of view.

Projective stage: Piaget's second stage of spatial development. It includes the development of perspective, the ability to understand how things appear from different points of view.

Scale: A ratio specifying the relationship of the distance between points on a map to the distance between corresponding points in the real world, such as one inch on the map equals ten miles in the area mapped.

Side elevation: The view, usually of a structure, along a line perpendicular to the side of the structure.

Symbol: An image used in the map of a space to represent an object in that space.

Technology: The artifacts, systems, and environments designed by people to improve their lives.

Topological stage: Piaget's first stage of spatial development in which children construct qualitative spatial relationships such as nearness, order, separation, and being open/closed.